Financial Markets: An Introduction

Rob Dixon
Senior Lecturer – Durham University Business School
Durham, UK

and

Phil Holmes
Lecturer in Finance, Durham University, Durham, UK

CHAPMAN & HALL
University and Professional Division

London · Glasgow · Weinheim · New York · Tokyo · Melbourne · Madras

Published by Chapman & Hall, 2–6 Boundary Row, London SE1 8HN, UK

Chapman & Hall, 2–6 Boundary Row, London SE1 8HN, UK

Blackie Academic & Professional, Wester Cleddens Road, Bishopbriggs, Glasgow G64 2NZ, UK

Chapman & Hall, 29 West 35th Street, New York NY10001, USA

Chapman & Hall Japan, Thomson Publishing Japan, Hirakawacho Nemoto Building, 6F, 1-7-11 Hirakawacho, Chiyoda-ku, Tokyo 102, Japan

Chapman & Hall Australia, Thomas Nelson Australia, 102 Dodds Street, South Melbourne, Victoria 3205, Australia

Chapman & Hall India, R. Seshadri, 32 Second Main Road, CIT East, Madras 600 035, India

First edition 1992
First published in paperback 1995

© 1992 Rob Dixon and Phil Holmes

Phototypeset in 11/13 Palatino by Intype, London
Printed in Great Britain by TJ Press (Padstow) Ltd, Padstow

ISBN 0 412 62280 7

A catalogue record for this book is available from the British Library

Library of Congress Cataloging-in-Publication data available

To J. R. Farley for inspiring the constant search for understanding

Contents

Preface

The increasing complexity of financing business activity has drawn many managers into a web of jargon with no apparent escape. The purpose of this book is to give students and hard pressed managers ready access to the terminology of finance and an insight into many of the key financial instruments.

The book's key aim is to increase the level of understanding of the processes and techniques of finance and financial markets. The aim is derived from many conversations with managers keen to understand financing and risk management techniques open to their business.

The strength of the book is that it makes apparently complex financial markets understandable and as a consequence approachable.

The authors are grateful to J. Barnes for his assistance and helpful comments on earlier versions of four chapters, and Alan Nelson and Sarah Henderson for their quiet and persistent cajoling.

CHAPTER ONE

Introduction

In recent years the presentation of movements in financial markets and, more particularly, the reporting of items of financial news have become regular and frequent features of radio, television, and newspaper reporting. The events surrounding the stock market crash of 1987, the so called 'Guinness affair', and the dealings of the Bank of Credit and Commerce International have hit the headlines and been the subject of many hours of broadcasting time and many column inches of newspaper reporting.

However, reporting of financial news and details of financial markets is not restricted to the issues surrounding such obviously financial activities. Such reporting takes place, and indeed is given considerable prominence in the media, when events which appear to be far removed from financial markets occur. So, for example, the resignation of Mrs Thatcher as Prime Minister in the UK was accompanied by details of the impact of her resignation on the stock market and the foreign exchange markets. Similarly, the invasion of Kuwait by Iraq and the subsequent proceedings in the Gulf War impacted on financial markets in a newsworthy way.

Indeed, the effect on financial markets of what appear to be purely political activities can be very dramatic. For example, on 20 August 1991 the *Guardian* reported that 'The world's financial markets were plunged into chaos yesterday by news of the *coup* which ousted President Gorbachev. . . . In London £16 billion was wiped off share values.' This led to 19 August being named 'Red Monday'. In addition, the coup had a very significant impact on exchange rates. The announcement of the failure of the *coup* three days later triggered countermovements in the financial markets which were once again widely reported.

Clearly, then, financial markets are 'big news' and are affected by events which at first sight do not appear to be related to those markets. Nevertheless, while the details of financial markets are newsworthy it is questionable whether there is a widespread understanding of the markets. From a manager's point of view it is essential that these markets are understood since changes in, for example, the exchange rate between Germany and the UK can have a considerable impact on the profitability of a business or the desirability of pursuing a particular investment or contract. Indeed, the fact that the pound sterling rose more than three pfennigs against the German mark on the day of the *coup* in the USSR could be sufficient to transform a highly profitable enterprise into a loss-making activity. It should be evident that there is a need for managers to gain an understanding of the financial environment in which their organization operates and of the system of financial markets which are available to them.

One of the main problems in trying to come to an understanding of financial markets lies in the fact that there has been very considerable change in these markets over the last quarter of a century. The late 1960s witnessed a period of increasing pressure on the foreign exchange rate system set up at the end of the Second World War with the agreement reached at Bretton Woods in 1944. This pressure intensified to the extent that in the early 1970s there was a breakdown in the fixed exchange rate regime and the introduction of floating exchange rates. This change, together with other major economic events such as the rapid rise in oil prices in 1973–4, led to managers and firms facing greatly increased uncertainty in the environment in which they operated.

In response to this greater uncertainty, and in particular to the increased volatility in exchange rates and interest rates, financial markets further developed means by which managers and firms could manage the risks they faced. Of particular significance in this regard was the introduction of derivative financial markets such as futures and options in the first half of the 1970s. These markets have grown substantially since their introduction and are now an important means for hedging risks.

The rapid developments which took place in the 1970s were followed by a period of further significant change in the 1980s, although the nature of this change was somewhat different. The most striking feature of the financial system in the 1980s has been the introduction of deregulation and the liberalization of financial markets. In the UK this process of deregulation led to the 'Big Bang' of October 1986, which altered the means by which equities and gilt-edged securities were traded. These securities are now traded through a system of computers rather than through the old method of trading on the floor of the Stock Exchange. Clearly, such a move was aided by developments in computer technology over the last two decades.

Concomitant with this period of deregulation was the move towards 'popular capitalism' in the UK. Under the Conservative Government elected in 1979 and in power throughout the 1980s, a policy of privatization has been implemented. This resulted in the massive flotation of enterprises which were previously in the public sector, with many of the shareholders of the privatized companies being new to share ownership.

The 1980s also saw further substantial volatility in foreign exchange markets. For example, the exchange rate between the pound sterling and the US dollar has fluctuated between a situation of virtual parity (£1 = $1) and $2.40 to the pound. There is no evidence to suggest that this volatility will fall in future years. Indeed, in the first six months of 1991 the rate varied from approximately $2 to the pound to $1.60 to the pound.

The other memorable event of the 1980s in terms of financial markets is the stock market crash of October 1987, when billions of pounds were wiped off the value of securities in a matter of hours. For many of the investors new to stock markets as a result of the privatization policy, the crash came as a sudden and unpleasant shock. In addition, it impacted on business confidence and led to an easing of Government policy which has been blamed for subsequent inflation in the UK economy and elsewhere.

The 1990s look like being a period of equally dramatic events and developments in the financial system. In 1990 the UK joined the Exchange Rate Mechanism of the European Monetary System, only to leave again two years later. Political events in 1990 and 1991 have already had significant effects on financial markets and further privatizations are possible in the UK.

In the light of the rapid change which has taken place over the last twenty-five years and the likely developments in the future it is not easy to come to terms with the financial system. However, financial markets impact on the operations and profitability of all organizations, and it is therefore essential that managers gain an understanding of these markets. This holds true for managers at all levels within a firm. It is simply not the case that managers can leave an understanding of financial markets to company accountants or financial advisers.

In order to help managers gain an understanding of financial markets, the way in which those markets impact on the performance of firms, and the way in which the markets can be used to help to meet company objectives, this book examines the relevant major markets. However, the authors believe that, in order to benefit fully from a knowledge of financial markets, it is necessary to be able to put the workings of those markets into context. For that reason, this introduction is followed by a chapter on financial market efficiency, which briefly explains the role of financial markets and discusses the notion of market efficiency, essentially demonstrating the reliability of the signals sent out by the markets. In addition, the significance and implications of financial market efficiency are explained. Chapters 3 and 4 explain the main sources of funds for firms by examining the stock market and markets for debt capital. Chapter 5 is concerned with Euromarkets, which have developed considerably over recent years and which are playing an increasingly important role in the financial system. Venture capital is the subject of Chapter 6 as, although still representing a small proportion of total funds, venture capital is of importance to many firms which are unable to attract finance from more traditional sources. Foreign exchange markets are examined in Chapter 7, with emphasis being placed on the way in which managers can deal with the risks associated with foreign exchange transactions. The final two chapters introduce and explain the two main derivative markets, futures and options. The role of these markets as a means of risk management is examined.

In addition to explaining the main characteristics of each of the markets considered and putting these markets in context by the explanation of the issue of financial market efficiency, emphasis is placed on the importance of these markets for managers. Hence, the practical use of these markets is stressed, as is the role of the markets as a means of risk management. It should thus become clear that far from being a 'rich man's casino' where great fortunes are won and lost as a result of chance, financial markets provide a very useful source of funds and provide an important means of risk management.

CHAPTER TWO

The efficiency of financial markets

INTRODUCTION

This chapter is concerned with the efficiency of financial markets and, in particular, the efficient markets hypothesis. It may appear strange that a book which is designed to provide an introduction to financial markets should begin with a chapter concerning a hypothesis. However, there are good grounds for including a chapter on the efficient markets hypothesis in a book such as this. In particular, it is possible to identify three main reasons for discussing the meaning and implications of the efficient markets hypothesis (EMH).

1. The ENH dispels some misplaced and misguided beliefs about financial markets. In particular, by showing that security prices are based on relevant available information, it dispels the view that operating in financial markets is a gamble akin to betting in a casino.
2. Knowledge of the EMH leads managers who are considering carrying out transactions in financial markets to ask the relevant questions about the nature of those markets.
3. The EMH offers firm advice for the behaviour of managers and investors who operate in financial markets.

Hence, it can be seen that the EMH is potentially of great importance in gaining an understanding of financial markets. For this reason a book which aims to provide a guide to such markets would be lacking if it did not set those markets in context by explaining the EMH.

The issue of the efficiency of financial markets is not concerned with the question of whether the participants in those markets work hard each day. Rather, the efficiency of the markets refers to the way in which prices are set in the markets and the information which is used in setting those prices. In order to understand the EMH it is helpful to consider the role of financial markets.

THE ROLE OF FINANCIAL MARKETS

One of the fundamental roles of financial markets is to transfer funds between different economic units (for example, households and firms). This transfer of funds takes place between two groups.

1. There are economic units which have savings but which do not have 'real' investment opportunities ('real' investment means opportunities to invest in productive activities). Households are the main source of these 'savings surplus' economic units. For example, households do not typically have the opportunity to invest directly in a productive activity of their own; rather, their savings are channelled into productive investment by, perhaps, saving with a bank or building society, or the purchase of shares in a company.
2. There are economic units which have productive opportunities but which do not have the funds necessary to undertake these 'real' investments. These 'savings deficit' economic units are typically firms.

The role of financial markets is to bring these two groups together so that a transfer of funds can take place from savings surplus units to savings deficit units. The effect of this transfer is to enable productive opportunities to be undertaken that, in the absence of financial markets, might otherwise have to be rejected. For example, a company which wishes to build a factory to produce a new product might not have the funds necessary to complete the building. Similarly, Ms Smith may have money she wishes to save but no opportunity to invest productively. By purchasing new shares in the company Ms Smith has indirectly invested in a productive opportunity and the company can go ahead with its plans to build the factory (with the help of a great many other investors).

In a situation where there are 'well-functioning' financial markets, both borrowers and lenders in the markets are made better off as a result of the existence of the markets. Ms Smith is better off because she can indirectly invest in productive opportunities and get a return on her investment, and the company is better off because it can undertake the investment.

From the lender's point of view, the crucial question regarding their investment is, 'Will the returns from the investment compensate me for the risk which I incur?' On the other side, the borrower wants to be sure that the cost of the funds being raised is reasonable. It is the role of the financial markets not only to receive signals from potential borrowers and lenders about such things as the risk of any investment and the rate of return required by investors to compensate them for that risk, but also to interpret accurately those signals. If this happens then both lenders and borrowers can be sure that the markets price securities in a way which accurately reflects the risk associated with the security, and managers can be sure that in raising capital for a company they are paying a reasonable price for the funds.

In such a situation the prices of securities will be such that they represent the best possible estimate of the worth of the securities and there will be no 'good buys', or securities that are underpriced. Of vital importance for all market participants, and in particular for managers who need to raise funds, is the question of whether the markets can be expected to price securities in such a way that there are no good buys. In practice, there are good reasons why it might be expected that this will be the case. Most importantly, financial markets are typically characterized by a considerable amount of competition. This competition exists both in the demand for funds (in addition to there being very many companies seeking to raise funds, local authorities and central government look to the financial markets for money) and in the supply of funds. Of particular importance on the supply side is the fact that there are very many investment analysts either investing funds on their own behalf or acting on behalf of other investors. These analysts all operate with the aim of obtaining as high a return as possible on any investments they make (either for themselves or for others). Hence, investment analysts are continually looking for a security that is underpriced. In attempting to discover underpriced securities they gain access to a considerable volume of information about the security and about the prospects for that security. In searching out this information it might be expected that the analysts find out all that is relevant to the price of the security and, through their actions, lead security prices to reflect the true worth of the asset. In other words the intense competition to find underpriced securities might lead to there being no securities which are, in fact, underpriced.

The important question is whether this intense competition among analysts leads to financial markets being 'efficient'. In order to address this question it is necessary to be more specific about the meaning of the term 'efficient'.

THE EFFICIENCY OF FINANCIAL MARKETS

The efficiency of financial markets is primarily concerned with the availability of information in those markets. In particular, for a financial market to be described as efficient, information about the securities traded in that market should be accessible to market participants at relatively low cost. In addition, the prices of securities being traded should incorporate all the relevant information which can be acquired.

There are two aspects to the efficiency of financial markets.

Operational efficiency   requires that the participants supplying and demanding funds be able to carry out transactions cheaply.

If the system of financial intermediaries is very competitive then the price of the services of these intermediaries will tend to be low and markets will be operationally efficient. In practice, there is considerable competition in most developed financial markets and markets are thus typically efficient in this sense.

Allocational efficiency   requires the prices of securities to be such that they equalize the risk-adjusted rates of return across all securities. This means that prices will be set so that securities with the same level of risk will offer the same expected return. In a market which is allocationally efficient, savings are allocated to productive investment in an optimal way and all participants in the market benefit.

The two types of efficiency are not unlinked. It is important to recognize that, without operational efficiency, allocational efficiency is much less likely. When new information becomes available about a particular security (it may be announced, for example, that an oil company has discovered a major new oilfield) then we would expect the price of that security to change (in this case to rise) as people seek to either sell or (in this case) buy that security in response to the new information. If there are high transaction costs then there is a barrier to buying and selling, because the potential gains from acquiring the security would be wiped out (at least in part) by the transaction costs. Hence, since there is a barrier to transactions taking place, there is a barrier to savings moving to their new optimal allocation. Operational inefficiency can thus lead to allocational inefficiency.

BACKGROUND TO THE EMH

The EMH is primarily concerned with allocational efficiency. According to the EMH, financial markets are efficient if security prices fully reflect all relevant information as soon as that information becomes available. If they do, then the prices of securities are accurate signals for the allocation of savings.

It is helpful in trying to explain the EMH to examine its history. The EMH really emerged as a result of the findings of investigations carried out by a statistician, Maurice Kendall. Kendall had set out to examine the price behaviour of stocks and commodities in the expectation that he would be able to discover regular patterns in those prices. The results of his work (published in 1953) surprised not only Kendall but also many economists. Kendall discovered that stock and commodity prices did not follow regular patterns, but rather prices appeared to change at random. (The term used to describe this price behaviour was 'random walk'.) The main implication of Kendall's work was that no information could be gained on the price that a security will trade at in the future by examining past prices.

In response to this finding, many economists and statisticians carried out further work in an attempt to discover price patterns. Price patterns were not discovered, however, and evidence to support Kendall's findings grew.

The considerable volume of evidence which was accumulated showing that price changes are random appeared to suggest that there was no logic to the way in which prices are set. However, on further consideration it can be seen that apparently random price behaviour is to be expected in a financial market characterized by considerable competition. In a competitive market, analysts are continually searching for good buys, and in doing so will have discovered everything that there is to know concerning the worth of the security. The price of a security would thus reflect all available information, and in this situation the only time that the price would change is when new information becomes available. Since, by definition, it is not possible to predict new information, then price changes also cannot be predicted. Hence, price changes will only occur when new information becomes available and these changes will therefore appear to be random. Thus, far from lacking logic, random price changes are the logical result of competitive financial markets.

Indeed, the fact that analysts are constantly searching for price patterns to exploit means that, if one were identified, then it would immediately be destroyed by analysts trying to exploit it. For example, take the case where it is discovered that the price of Followpattern shares had risen on Mondays, Tuesdays, and Wednesdays and had then fallen on Thursdays for the last three weeks. If this week the price of the shares is seen to rise on Monday and Tuesday and is still rising on Wednesday morning, then analysts will try to exploit the pattern they have identified. In order to do this they will seek to sell shares in Followpattern on Wednesday afternoon before the predicted fall on Thursday. However, identification of the pattern will lead to a large number of shares being sold on Wednesday afternoon, which will result in the price of Followpattern shares falling on Wednesday afternoon, rather than Thursday, and the pattern will have been destroyed.

This explanation of random security price movements only came in the wake of the findings of Kendall and the other statisticians and economists who researched security prices. The findings had initially come as a surprise to academics, and subsequent work concentrated on developing a fuller explanation of the price-setting behaviour of financial markets and the implications of this behaviour for the users of the markets. One of the early results of this work was the development of the efficient markets hypothesis.

THE EFFICIENT MARKETS HYPOTHESIS

A financial market is said to be efficient if prices fully reflect all the information which is available and which is relevant to security valuation. In other words, the set of prices arrived at in the market reflect all that is known about the securities.

This will include information on company earnings (both past and expected future earnings), dividend levels (again, past and those expected in the future), gearing or leverage, expected growth rates, and the level of risk of the company. In addition, factors such as the state of industrial relations in a company or the health of senior managers can affect the price of securities, and any information relating to such items should also be incorporated into security prices. An example of the health of senior managers affecting security prices is where, perhaps, the founder of a company has retained overall control but is viewed as being a liability to the growth and future profitability of the company. If he or she were to become ill and have to relinquish control then the fortunes of the company may be expected to improve. Hence, if information became available that the founder was seriously ill, then in an efficient market a rational response to such news could be to see an increase in the value of the company's stock.

For a market to be efficient the requirement that prices fully reflect all available relevant information must hold true at all times. Given this requirement, it follows that, for a market to be efficient, any new information must be incorporated into security prices immediately and accurately. This means that a response to new information (whether it be finding out that an oil company has discovered a major new oilfield or learning of the serious illness of the founder of a company) in terms of a price adjustment must be both almost instantaneous and of a direction and size which fully reflects the significance of the information.

If a financial market is characterized by almost instantaneous adjustments to new information, and if the responses are of the relevant direction and size, then when new information which is thought to be good news for the company becomes available the only investors who will benefit from it will be people who happen to be holding the shares of that company at the time the information is disclosed. Similarly, bad news will adversely affect the holders of the security at the time of the disclosure. In other words, in an efficient market the response of the market to new information precludes people from trading profitably on the basis of that information. In particular, the response to new information will be such that when good news is disclosed people not holding the security at the time of disclosure will only be able to purchase the security at a price which has taken account of the good news.

Equally, the holders of shares in a company for which bad news is disclosed will only be able to sell the shares at a price which takes account of the bad news.

In short, investors will not be able to make regular superior returns. In such a situation, the only ways that investors can earn above-average returns is either by investing in high-risk securities which will offer above-average returns, or by chance (they happen to be holding shares in the oil company, for example, when discovery of the new oilfield is disclosed). If a market were not efficient then astute investors would have time to trade profitably from the disclosure of new information.

THE THREE LEVELS OF MARKET EFFICIENCY

In defining market efficiency, reference has so far been made to markets fully reflecting *all* relevant available information. However, the set of information which was used by Kendall was not *all* relevant information, but only that relating to past security prices. In order to make a distinction between markets which are efficient in relation to past security prices and those which are efficient in relation to other sets of information, three different levels of efficiency have been defined.

Weak form efficiency   A market is weak form efficient if security prices fully reflect the information contained in past price movements. In other words, security prices do not follow patterns which repeat, and this means that it is not possible to trade profitably purely on the basis of historical price information. This level of efficiency is the one which corresponds to Kendall's findings of a random walk.

Semistrong form efficiency   A market is semistrong form efficient if security prices fully reflect all publicly available information. Examples of such information is that contained in company annual reports, earnings and dividend announcements, changes in accounting practices, announcements regarding the ill health of the founder of the company, and so on. If a market is semistrong form efficient then investors cannot make superior returns by 'searching out' information from publicly available sources, since the information will already be incorporated into security prices.

Strong form efficiency   A market is strong form efficient if security prices fully reflect all relevant information whether it is publicly available or not. In this situation no investor could ever earn consistently superior returns; even an insider could not trade profitably from inside knowledge.

There is a link between the three levels of efficiency. If a market is semistrong form efficient then it must also be weak form efficient, because past prices (the basis of weak form efficiency) are publicly available information (the basis of semistrong form efficiency). Similarly, if a market is strong form efficient then it must also be semistrong form and weak form efficient. This is because strong form efficiency requires that all information (including that publicly available) is reflected in security prices. However, it is of course possible for a market to be weak form efficient and not efficient in either of the other two senses, or semistrong form efficient but not strong form efficient.

It should be clear that strong form efficiency is extremely demanding. Strong form efficiency requires that whenever anybody at all becomes aware of new information the market should instantaneously and in an unbiased fashion respond to that information. Intuition tells us that, in practice, this level of efficiency will not be attained. However, this does not imply that the EMH is meaningless. For the vast majority of participants in the financial markets, and particularly for managers using the markets in their work, the availability of inside information is limited in the extreme. Hence, for most participants it is not the strong form of efficiency which is relevant, but rather the semistrong form. If markets are efficient in the semistrong sense then for most investors the markets are, for all practical purposes, efficient.

THE ROLE OF THE EXPERT INVESTMENT ANALYST

The presence of investment analysts is one of the reasons why financial markets do not develop price patterns which repeat. In order for investment analysts to feel that it is worthwhile trying to seek out price patterns (or any other information relevant to security valuation) there must be a belief that financial markets are inefficient. Indeed, there is a strong view among practitioners that financial markets *are* inefficient.

It is possible to identify three main types of investment analyst.

Technical analysts   These analysts determine investment strategies on the basis of past share price information. While there are two types of technical analyst, they both work on the basis that it is possible to trade profitably by using past share price data, and hence both types can be seen as viewing markets to be weak form inefficient. Firstly, there are chartists, who analyse charts or graphs of share price movements in the hope of identifying patterns which can be used to forecast future price movements. The other type of technical analyst devises mechanical trading rules. For example, some use filter rules which are aimed at buying shares before they reach a high level and sell before lower levels are achieved. The principle behind these rules is that there are identifiable patterns in security price movements which can be exploited.

Fundamental analysts   As the name suggests, these analysts study the fundamentals of companies, such as past earnings, dividends, gearing, and the like, with the aim of forecasting future returns and the true worth of the security. They believe that undervalued securities can then be identified, purchased, and held until the price moves to the true worth value. Given that the basis of fundamental analysts' research is publicly available information, they are clearly working on the assumption that markets are semistrong form inefficient.

Insider dealers   These dealers try to obtain information which is not publicly available, in the hope of trading profitably before the information reaches the market and is taken into account in the price of securities. Insider dealers are working on the basis that markets are strong form inefficient. Since the Companies Act 1980, insider dealing is illegal in the UK.

While all these analysts trade on the assumption that financial markets are inefficient, there is a vast amount of evidence to suggest that these markets are in fact efficient, at least at the semistrong level. (This evidence will be discussed in the next section.) The irony of this situation is that it is likely that it is the activities of analysts which cause markets to be efficient. If they cease their activities financial markets are more likely to become inefficient. Thus, the paradox appears to be that the very people whose activities are based on the view that the market is inefficient actually help to bring about the efficiency of those markets.

THE EVIDENCE OF EFFICIENCY

Since Kendall's findings were first made public there has been an extremely large amount of research conducted into examining the efficiency of financial markets. While much of the early work concentrated on trying to find patterns in share price movements, and was thus testing markets for weak form efficiency, in later years considerable testing of the semistrong and, to a lesser extent, the strong forms of efficiency has been carried out.

Given this large volume of evidence, it is not possible to discuss the results in detail here. However, while there have been literally hundreds of tests of market efficiency, the findings of these tests have been little short of unanimous. Almost without exception there is evidence that financial markets are, for all practical purposes, very largely efficient at the weak and semistrong levels. While technically some inefficiencies have been discovered, their exploitation would require very frequent trading, with the result that any potential gains from trading on the basis of these inefficiencies would be wiped out by transaction costs.

There is some evidence to suggest that markets are strong form inefficient (though evidence of this nature is difficult to find, given the private nature of much of the information and the fact that insider trading is illegal). However, since there is overwhelming evidence of efficiency at the semistrong level, then for the vast majority of market participants, and for managers wishing to use these markets, the assumption of efficiency appears to be warranted. The existence of efficient financial markets has important implications for the behaviour of managers wishing to use those markets.

THE IMPLICATIONS OF MARKET EFFICIENCY

The efficient markets hypothesis is not something which is of purely academic interest. EMH has important implications for the behaviour of anybody who is contemplating operating in financial markets. As far as managers are concerned it is possible to identify a number of implications arising from the hypothesis.

There is no optimal time to issue new securities
In an inefficient market the prices of securities will sometimes be at a level which does not reflect the true worth of those securities. Hence, when companies want to issue new capital they will only wish to do so if the market price of the securities is at or above the true market value. If securities are underpriced then by issuing securities at that time the company would raise capital of less than the true worth of the securities issued.

Therefore, in an inefficient market, a company wishing to make new issues at a time of underpricing would be better off waiting until the price of the securities reaches the true value. In relation to this it is sometimes believed that when the market as a whole has gone through a period of falling prices it is unwise to issue new capital. Rather the company should wait until prices have picked up.

However, if markets are efficient then this argument is fallacious, since prices will *always* reflect the true worth of the security. Hence, it is pointless to wait for 'the guaranteed increase in prices' to issue new capital. As has been shown, if a rise in prices was indeed guaranteed then the price would increase immediately. The important implication of this is that there is no optimal time for the issue of new securities in an efficient market. Even if prices are at a historically low level it does not mean that they will definitely rise in the near future.

Nevertheless, there is one exception to this general rule. If a market is semistrong form efficient but strong form inefficient, then it may be beneficial for a company to delay an issue if it is aware of relevant (inside) information concerning the company. If good news is known to the company (the discovery of the oilfield) then it should seek to transmit this information to the market prior to the new issue.

Do not buy apparently undervalued companies

The takeover of one company by another can take place for many sound economic reasons. For example, it might be felt that the full potential of a company is not being utilized under its present management, or that it would benefit from joining forces with a larger firm operating in a related field. However, in addition to such sound reasons, there is another reason which is sometimes used to justify a takeover which, in an efficient market, is not at all sound.

One company will sometimes seek to take over another company for the sole reason that it believes that the market is undervaluing that company. Clearly, in an efficient market such a situation cannot arise, and so it is only if there are other reasons for takeover that a company should pursue such a policy. Managers who are told that a company is worth buying simply because it is undervalued should dismiss such advice.

Accept market prices as correct

The above discussion of takeovers essentially rests on the view that financial markets correctly price securities. A similar argument can be used to consider the policy adopted by management towards exchange rates and interest rates.

In order for an individual to outperform the market consistently, it is necessary for that individual to have more information than anybody else. Hence, managers who carry out transactions in markets for foreign currencies or interest-bearing securities should not work on the assumption that they are better at forecasting movements in exchange rates or interest rates than is the market. To do so in an efficient market would be at best pointless, and at worst extremely counterproductive.

You cannot fool efficient markets: issuing 'cheap' securities

In recent years many new types of securities have been introduced into financial markets. The idea behind some of these securities, such as convertibles, is that by combining characteristics of different types of securities (in this case debt and equity) it is possible for a company to pay less for its capital.

However, in an efficient market, securities such as convertibles will be priced on the basis of what they are, namely, a *mix* of debt and equity. Hence, although a convertible will be sold with a lower nominal interest rate than normal debt capital, this is for the simple reason that it is not normal debt capital. It is not possible to fool an efficient market.

You cannot fool efficient markets: stock splits

An increasingly common practice for firms is for them to carry out stock splits, by means of a scrip issue, for example, or by distributing shares as dividends. In an efficient market such a course of action will have no net impact on the firm's cash flows or on the cash flows to shareholders. An efficient market will simply revalue the shares to take account of the increased number of shares. For example, where a pre-split price of shares is £5 and one share is issued for every four held then the post-split price will be £4 per share. Thus, an individual who previously held 100 shares with a value of £500, will, after the scrip issue, hold 125 shares with a value of £500. It is not possible to fool an efficient market.

You cannot fool efficient markets: accounting practices

Over time, firms will typically change accounting practices. This is sometimes done because it is required by law, but sometimes it is done with the main purpose of trying to make investors believe that the company is doing better than it is – accounting practices may be changed to make earnings look higher, for example.

In an efficient market such changes will be seen for what they are, and the market will be able to isolate the impact of the change in practice. It is not possible to fool an efficient market.

Follow a passive investment strategy

The EMH implies that the price of any security is the best estimate of the true worth of that security at that time. This implies that investors should not waste time trying to identify underpriced securities as these simply do not exist. Hence, pursuing an active investment strategy which involves frequent changes in the securities held will not lead to superior returns being made, but rather will incur unnecessary transaction costs.

Given that some of the risk associated with any single investment can be removed by holding a diversified portfolio (for example, when one company is experiencing bad labour relations another will be going through a period of good labour relations), investors should buy a diversified portfolio of securities and hold on to that portfolio. In other words, they should follow a 'buy and hold' strategy, rather than a 'buy-hold-sell' strategy with all of its associated transaction costs.

MISCONCEPTIONS ABOUT THE EMH

A great many misguided beliefs are held about the EMH. Some represent a genuine misunderstanding of what EMH implies, others represent an attempt to undermine the hypothesis. It is sometimes maintained that financial market efficiency implies that the markets are able to forecast future prices perfectly, but EMH implies no such thing. Efficiency implies that security prices fully take account of the uncertainties of the future, rather than suggest that the future can be forecast with certainty.

Similarly, efficiency does not imply a lack of logic or rationality in the setting of security prices. Just because price movements are random does not mean that the markets are irrational. Indeed, random price movements imply rationality.

Another conclusion which is sometimes inaccurately drawn from the EMH is the view that investment analysts are fulfilling no useful function and are inefficient at their jobs. In reality the opposite is true. In an efficient market it is the ability of analysts to search out information which brings about efficiency, and hence they are fulfilling the function of enabling financial resources to be allocated to their best uses.

Efficiency does not imply that above-average risk-adjusted returns can never be earned. If it did it would be easy to disprove the EMH. The implication of efficiency is that it is not possible to make above-average risk-adjusted rates of return on a consistent basis. However, if an investor happens to be holding a security when good news is announced about the asset on which the security is written, then that investor will make above-average returns on that occasion. Equally, however, if the investor is holding securities when bad news is announced, then below-average returns will be earned. EMH tells us that in an efficient market superior (or indeed inferior) returns for a given level of risk can only be achieved by luck, not by skill.

It is important that, in trying to gain an understanding of the EMH and its implications for managerial behaviour, managers do not fall prey to these misconceptions.

CONCLUSION

If a full understanding of financial markets and the ways in which they can be used by managers is to be achieved, it is necessary to have some knowledge of the EMH. In some senses the EMH is a straightforward concept: it simply says that security prices fully reflect available relevant information. However, while the concept is fairly simple, it is sometimes difficult to believe that financial markets in practice can be efficient. Equally, the implications of efficiency are not always easy to take on board.

None the less, there is overwhelming evidence to support the view that financial markets are actually efficient, in spite of investment analysts' claims to the contrary. Hence, the concept of efficiency needs to be accepted, and the implications of the EMH for the behaviour of managers in financial markets understood and adhered to.

FURTHER READING

For an excellent and very readable discussion of EMH the following is recommended:

Keane, S.M. (1983) *Stock Market Efficiency*, Philip Allan, Oxford.

In addition, the following may be of interest:

Fama, E. (1970) 'Efficient capital markets: a review of theory and empirical work', in *Journal of Finance*, **25** (May), 383–417.

Fama, E. (1991) 'Efficient capital markets: II' in *Journal of Finance*, **46** (December), 1575–1617.

CHAPTER THREE

The Stock Exchange as a source of finance

Companies often find themselves in need of additional finance. Managers must be aware of the possibilities and difficulties of raising cash from the public, via the Stock Exchange. This chapter explains how the Stock Exchange works, and how companies may make the best use of the funds available.

BACKGROUND

In order to finance long-term projects, organizations require long-term finance. For example, investment in a new, sophisticated machine in a factory may not generate returns for a number of years. The use of the machine itself may not meet the costs of finance for the first two or three years, and thus long-term funding is required. If short-term funds were used, such as a bank overdraft, the company may have to sell the machine in order to pay off the debt should the overdraft be called in. Generally speaking, long-term finance refers to arrangements that provide for repayment over a period longer than ten years.

Long-term finance is available in a wide variety of forms, but there are three main types: variable income and capital investments, fixed income investments, and fixed capital investments. It is the first two of these that are available from the Stock Exchange. The most important investments with variable capital and income are ordinary shares, and the pre-

dominant fixed income investments are debentures and preference shares.

The Stock Exchange in London is the most important
capital market in the UK, and plays a very significant role in
the raising of funds for companies. Before looking more
closely at the workings of the Stock Exchange, it is necessary
to consider the pros and cons of capital markets generally.

THE CAPITAL MARKET

The term 'capital market' refers to the long-term market for
funds. This definition, however, is not strictly applied. In the
context of this chapter, 'capital market' may be defined as a
market where long-term negotiable securities are listed and
traded. There are three types of capital market securities: company securities (such as loan stock, shares, and options), public
sector securities (gilt-edged securities issued by governments
and well-established large firms), and Eurobonds.

The primary and secondary markets

These two facets of the capital market have distinct functions.
The primary market issues and deals in new securities. Thus
a company wishing to raise new equity on the Stock Exchange
'New Issues Market' is dealt with by the primary market. The
secondary market deals with existing financial claims. Dealing
on the secondary market does not raise new finance for the
quoted company, but rather enables the lender to transfer
the repayment rights to another, while the borrower remains
unaffected. However, the secondary market is important to
the borrower in that the secondary market enables the initial
investors to sell the investment as and when they choose.
Without the secondary market companies would find investors
less willing to tie up their money for extended periods, thus
making the raising of finance by share issue more difficult.

Effective primary and secondary markets

As already stated in Chapter 1, the prime function of the markets is to match lenders to borrowers and effect the directing of funds between them. In order to be efficient and effective in this activity, there are several characteristics which are to be desired.

1. The primary market, when operating efficiently, will present low transaction costs. The costs of legal fees, brokers' fees, and so on, effectively 'lose' part of the investment and could substantially increase the cost of raising finance.
2. Both primary and secondary markets should be efficient in the allocation of financial resources to the most productive uses.
3. Activity generated by the primary market should not be allowed to have a major impact upon shares in the secondary market. If this were to happen, then investors would obviously be less willing to invest in a company whose shares were falling. This effect can be minimized by ensuring that the volume of transactions in the secondary market is much greater than that in the primary market.
4. Secondary markets, while providing liquidity and flexibility for investors, are most likely to promote investment if they can reduce price volatility, and are efficient operationally, allocatively, and informationally.
5. The confidence of investors that they are not buying at an unfavourable price is boosted by eradicating large movements in share price. Reduced price volatility is achieved by greater activity in the market, depth, and breadth. 'Depth' refers to the number of buy and sell orders and how close they are to the current market price. If buy orders for shares with a market value of 100p are at 98p and 97p then these will support the price level. Conversely, if sell orders stand at 102p and 103p this also supports the price. This is because the share price cannot move far without activating the buy or sell orders which stabilize the price. 'Breadth' refers to the number of investors involved in the

market. If there is a wide range of investors, with varied motives, it is unlikely that all will decide to sell at the same time. Thus, breadth helps to reduce price volatility and further boosts the confidence of the investor.

6. As with the primary market, the operational efficiency of the secondary market refers to the transaction cost level. The major cost in the secondary market is known as the 'bid-ask spread' (the difference between the prices at which market makers are willing to buy and sell shares).

7. Allocative efficiency in the secondary market is achieved by the price mechanism. The investors need to be sure that the information provided by the secondary market regarding the directing of funds to the most productive uses is accurate, or they will not invest. Thus, the secondary market must also be informationally efficient. This requirement disables an individual investor from taking advantage of information that is not reflected in the share price. Informational efficiency implies that all relevant information is reflected in the share price.

THE STOCK EXCHANGE

The Stock Exchange functions as both a primary and a secondary market. As a source of finance the most significant function of the Stock Exchange is as a primary market. However, the secondary market of the Stock Exchange, as outlined above, is also valuable in support of the primary market, reinforcing investors' confidence in the purchase of a share issue.

There are four aspects of the Stock Exchange primary market. The first and largest market by far is the new issue market in gilts, and its considerable success in the sale of new gilts has enabled the Stock Exchange to help fund the Public Sector Borrowing Requirement (PSBR). The second, and a further example of the primary market raising funds for the Government, is privatization issues. The privatization policy of the Thatcher Government transformed state-owned assets into public limited companies. Shares in the new companies are issued and a listing on the Stock Exchange arranged.

Aspects three and four relate particularly to the private sector. The most successful primary market activity concerns the issue of new shares to existing shareholders, known as a rights issue. The fourth area of primary market activity is the raising of fixed interest capital for the private sector.

An area where the Stock Exchange has minimal activity is in the raising of new equity capital for new companies. One example of this absence is the case of North Sea exploration in the 1970s, which was financed by bank loans rather than share issues. More recently, the search for capital by EuroTunnel has led to a small proportion of the venture capital being raised by share issue, but this cannot be viewed as particularly successful, nor is this method common.

Gaining a quotation

Companies seeking finance from the stock market need to be prepared for a long and complicated process. The procedures can be baffling, with confusing related documentation, and companies with some sort of financial expertise will undoubtedly be better able to cope. When managers begin to consider the prospect of flotation advice should be sought about the company profile. Points of particular note in the profile are the last five years' performance as well as future forecasts in relation to attracting a sponsor, who will ultimately be responsible for the transition from private to public ownership and who would probably underwrite the issue of shares. The role of sponsor is most often filled by merchant banks or specialist stockbrokers.

In order to avoid the scramble which makes it very difficult for key decisions to be taken, particularly on forecasts, a reasonable lead time (about six months) must be planned into the flotation process. The lead time must not, on the other hand, be too long. If it is much longer than six months then a further set of interim accounts may be required, with the attendant extra costs and delays. The compilation of a 'long-form' report, usually by the company's auditors, for the sponsors will cover key areas of company activity, including: the nature of the business and the sector of operation; the competition; the company history and future outlook, including areas of risk and possible vulnerability; identification of specific dependence on individual customers or suppliers; and the quality of the management present and future.

Not all companies are in a position to use the Stock Exchange to raise finance. The first requirement is for the company to be quoted. In order to achieve this status the company must fulfil the requirements listed in the Stock Exchange's booklet *The Admission of Securities to Listing,* also known as 'The Yellow Book'. Complying with the requirements for listing clearly entails some cost.

1. Companies must meet the conditions for listing as laid down.
2. There are several methods of bringing securities to a listing. The method depends upon the type of security and the listing required.
3. There are specific listing requirements laid down by the Stock Exchange. The contents are laid down and include information about:
    (a) the person responsible for listing particulars, auditors, and other advisors;
    (b) the shares for which application is being made;
    (c) the issuer and its capital;
    (d) the group's activities;
    (e) the issuer's assets and liabilities;
    (f) the management;
    (g) the recent developments and prospects of the group;
    (h) general information about the issuer;
    (i) information about the certificates.
4. There are specific listing application procedures. Applications are considered every Wednesday and Friday. Some documents must be made available to the Exchange at least 14 days prior to the application, others 2 days before and others may be made on the day. Yet further documents may be submitted after the consideration date.

5. The listing particulars must be published and circulated. Prior to publication, however, they must be approved by the Exchange. Circulation has to be at a level to 'satisfy public demand' and is to be free of charge. Documents must be available for inspection and advertisements need approval and authorization.

6. Continuing obligations once a listing has been gained include:
   (a) the general obligation of disclosure;
   (b) notificaiton relating to capital;
   (c) notification of major interests in shares;
   (d) notification when the Company Announcements Office is not open for business;
   (e) rights as between holders of securities;
   (f) communication with shareholders; ñ R
   (g) other obligations.

7. The Stock Exchange has specific requirements for acquisitions and disposals by a listed company.

8. Restrictions governing current or recent directors (and their associates) are in place to prevent them taking advantage of their position.

9. The main financial details which need to be included in the listing particulars include:
   (a) comparative table and accountant's report;
   (b) profit forecast and estimate;
   (c) pro forma statements;
   (d) other financial statements outside the accountants report;
   (e) annual report and accounts;
   (f) summary financial statements;
   (g) half-yearly report.

10. Most documentation requires prior approval of the Exchange, but some do not. Items, which must still comply with the exchange requirements, but do not need prior approval include: memoranda and articles of association, trust deeds, employee's share schemes.

11. Overseas companies requiring a listing must comply with the listing rules, although there are some modifications

may be made depending on whether the Stock Exchange listing is a primary or secondary listing.

12. If the company own property or carries out certain property related transactions there are additional disclosure requirements which relate, principally, to valuations.
13. Mineral, oil and natural gas companies must submit a competent person's report as part of their application to a listing.
14. Scientific Research based companies have special requirements placed upon their applications. For example, such a company must intend to raise a minimum of £10 million pursuant to a marketing at the time of listing, and have a capitalization of at least £20m. Investment entities, public sector issuers, specialist debt securities and some others also have special rules applied.

This abbreviated list gives some indication of the sort of work involved in gaining a listing.

Advantages of a listing

Apart from the prestige that accompanies a Stock Exchange listing, there may be additional business generated by the increased status and credibility. If further finance is required at a later date, a further issue of shares (rights issue) may be made. This is a particularly cheap way of raising finance, as a dividend payout is not strictly required.

There are other advantages and some disadvantages associated with listing, but they do not directly relate to raising finance. Some disadvantages would include the higher level of disclosure required and the company receives a higher public profile which can make it more difficult for a company to ride periods of poor performance. The sharheolders' expectation of dividend payments can also exert pressure for a dividend policy that may not be in the best interests of the company.

Some companies are either too small or too new to gain a listing on the Stock Exchange, so to meet this the Stock Exchange set up the Unlisted Securities Market. The main feature is that the requirements for trading are lower than for a full listing. The USM is regarded as a stepping stone to full listing.

The main differences are that the company has to show a three-year record of trading and offer 10% of shares at the primary issue. There is no setting of a minimum capitalization, nor does the company have to provide an earnings forecast or a dividends policy for the year. The USM, whilst giving access to finance to medium-sized companies, does not significantly help smaller companies.

FINANCE AVAILABLE THROUGH THE STOCK EXCHANGE

Equity or ordinary shares

There are four main benefits to a company of issuing equity shares.

(a) There are no fixed charges associated with ordinary shares. While the company may pay a dividend if sufficient profits are generated, there is no obligation to do so.
(b) There is no fixed maturity date.
(c) They can provide a cushion against losses. On the occasion of a loss the sale of these shares increases the creditworthiness of the firm.
(d) They are usually more easily sold than debentures or preference shares because they carry a higher expected return. They therefore represent a better hedge against inflation.

The downside of ordinary share issues comes mainly from the costs and control aspects. The disadvantages include:

(a) The holders of new shares hold voting rights which could ultimately threaten the existing control structure of the company, which may be in the hands of owner/managers. For this reason it is unusual to see small or new companies being listed.
(b) Where there is profit distribution among ordinary shareholders, the profit will be spread over a wider group of people.
(c) Underwriting and distribution costs of new share issues are often very high. Thus, if there is a high proportion of equity capital then the overall cost of company capital is high.

Methods of issuing ordinary shares

Public issues by prospectus
The company, thorugh an agency issuing house, advertises the sale of shares in two London newspapers. In this method the

issuing house acts as the principal (that is, shares are issued direct to the public – see the section 'Offer for sale' below). The offer is accompanied by a prospectus (the preparation of the prospectus is probably the major flotation cost) in compliance with the Companies Act 1985. Alternatively, there may be the listing particulars, or information about where listing particulars may be found. The prospectus must include within it an accountant's report on the value of the business which is for sale.

Offer for sale

This is the usual method used when a large amount of capital is required. Such sales are often associated with the change from unlisted to listed status. This is similar in many ways to a public issue by prospectus, but the shares are actually sold to the issuing house, which then offers the shares to the public at a fixed price. The procedure requires that an application to issue a prospectus be made to the Committee on Quotations of the International Stock Exchange. Once the prospectus has been published, the company must wait two days before making a formal application to the Stock Exchange for a quotation.

Private placing

This method is used by unquoted companies for raising relatively small amounts of cash. Securities are marketed to specified persons or clients of the sponsor, or a securities house assisting in the policy. An offer to the public is not involved. The companies making use of this method usually intend to be quoted on the Stock Exchange in the future. The main cost saving comes from sub-underwriting, much advertising not being required.

Issue by tender

With this method the company offers shares to the public without specifying a price. The potential investors are invited to name the price they are willing to pay, though there is a lower price limit below which the shares will not be sold. The company clearly cannot know at what price the shares will eventually be sold. Investors, who will know the lower limit, may, if they choose, offer to buy the shares at a price higher than this. Different investors may offer different prices. All those offering a higher price than the lower limit will receive shares, although numbers may be scaled down if there is excess demand. Usually a single 'striking price' is fixed, although occasionally there is more than one price. All investors pay the striking price, even those who have offered to pay more. This method is particularly useful where it is uncertain what the price of a company's shares should be.

COSTS OF ISSUING SHARES

There are two facts regarding flotation that should be borne in mind. The first is that the cost of flotation for ordinary shares is greater than that for fixed-interest stocks. The second is that the cost of offers for sale as a percentage of gross proceeds is smaller than the cost of placings.

One reason for the first situation is that securities of the fixed-interest type are usually bought in large blocks by relatively few investors, usually of the institutional investor type. In contrast, ordinary shares tend to be bought in small numbers by a large number of small investors, probably individuals. Furthermore, the risks involved in underwriting ordinary shares are higher than those of fixed-interest securities, and so the underwriting costs are higher.

In the second case, because there are certain fixed expenses associated with any issue of securities, and because these expenses are relatively high, then the costs of issue as a percentage of gross proceeds is going to be greater in the case of a small issue, such as a placing. Furthermore, small issues tend to be undertaken by small, less well-known firms, and as a consequence the underwriting costs may be higher because there is an increased danger of leaving out vital information. It is possible for larger companies to reduce flotation costs by making use of rights issues.

Clearly, the costs of issue must be taken into account when deciding upon the sum to be raised, because the issue costs will have a bearing upon the cost of capital. The costs, which include underpricing, underwriting fees, capital duties payable, Stock Exchange listing fee, legal and broker's fees, advertising, printing, and so forth, have been studied and calculated as a percentage of the amount raised. The *Bank of England Quarterly Bulletin* published the figures shown in Table 3.1, which demonstrate that costs as a proportion of the sum raised varies considerably with the size of the issue.

Table 3.1 Average expenses as a percentage of amounts raised through share issues

Issue size and method	Listed market: new issue costs 1983–6 (quarter 1)	USM: new issue costs 1984–5
Up to £3m		
Placings	17.0	20.5
Offers for sale	14.2	16.4
Tenders	2.1	17.5
Subscriptions	–	30.6
£3m–£5m		
Placings	10.1	–
Offers for sale	27.0	17.0
Tenders	18.4	–
Subscriptions	(21.2)	–
£5m–£10m		
Placings	–	–
Offers for sale	10.9	(3.8)
Tenders	17.5	–
Subscriptions	–	–
Over £10m		
Placings	–	–
Offers for sale	9.2	(6.1)
Tenders	11.0	–
Subscriptions	(1.4)	–

Note: Where negative issue costs arise, costs in the form of fees have been more than offset by overpricing the issue.
Source: *Bank of England Quarterly Bulletin*, December, 1986, pp. 532–42

Rights issues

For companies listed on the Stock Exchange, rights issues are the most common method of issuing shares. Basically, a rights issue is an issue of new shares to existing shareholders in proportion to the shares they already hold. That is to say, existing shareholders are invited to subscribe cash for new shares. Rights issues are attractive to both the company and the existing shareholders. The company benefits from lower issue costs, in that administration and underwriting costs are lower and the issue is made at the discretion of the directors rather than via a general meeting of the company. This is because issues of equity through the Stock Exchange will alter the balance of ownership. The main attraction of the rights issue for current shareholders is that they are able to maintain their original proportion of share ownership. Furthermore, any transfer of wealth away from them, due to an equity issue being underpriced, is avoided. The principal disadvantage of the rights issue is that it has to be underwritten. This presents no problem unless the issue is not fully taken up by the shareholders and shares are left in the hands of the underwriters, which is, in effect, a vote of no confidence in the directors by the shareholders and the stock market.

In order to make a rights issue the company, when making the offer, must detail the reasons for the issue, the terms of the offer, the capital structure of the company at the time of issue, the future prospects for the company, and forecasts of future dividends. The timing of the issue, although started at the discretion of the directors, is governed eventually by the queuing system of the Stock Exchange.

Reasons for a rights issue

There are four main reasons why a company may choose to embark upon a rights issue.

1. When inflation is high, the company requires a greater cash resource to maintain the same volume of assets, in terms of

plant, machinery, stocks, and so on, due to the effect inflation has on the replacement costs of these assets. Unless the company can retain cash from substantial profits, the only alternative is to raise cash from a fresh issue of shares.

2. When the company is in a position to expand, additional cash resources are again required to fund the expansion. Expansion entails asset acquisition, and while current assets *may* also increase, the company may well ask shareholders for further cash to enable the expansion plans to be achieved. Some increase in cash may be possible through additional credit, but a larger capital base is often required as well.

3. If a company has a high proportion of interest-bearing loan capital (interest on which is payable whether or not profits are made) compared with shareholders' funds, then it is said to be 'highly geared', and in this position the company can suffer from a squeeze on profits. The company can improve the balance sheet by obtaining extra share capital via a rights issue (shares on which dividends are not obligatory when profits do not warrant them).

4. The fourth reason for rights issues was particularly prevalent in the mid–1980s. The rights issues of this period included a large number of issues which may be termed opportunist. At a time when share prices were relatively high, companies found it easy to persuade their shareholders to subscribe cash for new issues with a view to expansion by takeover. An example of this is the 1985 Hanson Trust rights issue which was made specifically to finance the takeovers of other companies. This particular rights issue raised £503 million net of expenses. The records for rights issues were broken in 1986 when a total of 186 companies raised some £4.5 billion.

Rights issue: calculations

There are a number of calculations that may be done in preparation for an issue and while many of these are primarily of interest to the shareholder, the company has to consider them closely. The first calculation is that of the amount that can be raised. The total amount that can be raised by an issue depends upon the rate that the market capitalizes earnings for the type of company issuing the shares, as well as the expected earnings on the new funds. Clearly, the funds raised by the new issue must at least increase the market value of the company by the amount of the funds raised. If this was not achieved the shareholders' wealth would be diminished.

The rights issue has to be priced in a way to make it attractive to existing shareholders, and it must therefore be priced below the current market price for the shares. However, the price must not be set too low, due to the adverse effects on earnings per share. Thus, in calculating the number of shares to issue to raise a given sum, account is taken of the resulting reduction of earnings per share at various issue prices. In practice, the most common pricing mechanism is to apply a discount of 15–20% to the current market price.

In theory, the effect of a rights issue on the share price is to reduce it a little, but it should be above the price at which the shares are offered. The ex-rights price can be calculated as a weighted average of the price of the rights and the pre-issue price. Thus, assuming that the rate of return remains unchanged:

$$\text{Ex-rights price} = Pp \; \frac{No}{N} + Pn \; \frac{Nn}{N}$$

where Pp = pre-issue price
Pn = new-issue price
No = number of old shares
Nn = number of new shares
N = total number of shares = $No + Nn$

Example A company has 8000 shares issued and the market price is £2 per share. The decision is made to issue a further 6000 shares at a price of £1.75.

The theoretical ex-rights price, using the formula above is:

$$\text{Ex-rights price} = \pounds2 \times \frac{8000}{14\,000} + \pounds1.75 \times \frac{6000}{14\,000} = \pounds1.89$$

Shareholders' Gain

The shareholder is able to calculate the theoretical gain from exercising the right using the formula:

$$\frac{\text{Market price (ex-rights)} - \text{Rights price}}{\text{Number of rights needed to gain one new share}}$$

Example   The basis for a rights issue is one new share for every five held. The new shares are being offered for £2.50 each, and the theoretical ex-rights price is £3.75. The value of each right may be calculated using the formula above.

$$\frac{\pounds3.75 - \pounds2.50}{5} = \pounds0.25$$

Whether a shareholder is able to gain or lose from the issue depends upon what the individual does with the issue. The options open to the shareholder include selling the rights on the open market, take up some or all of the entitlement to shares, or do nothing (allowing the right to lapse). Say a company has a total issued share capital of 500 000 shares at a nominal value of £1 each, and the current market value of each share is £1.35. The company wishes to raise finance for expansion; the directors have determined that they need to raise £125 000 and announce a rights issue. The basis of the rights issue is one new share for every four already held, at the nominal value. Our shareholder owns 500 shares, so 125 extra shares can be applied for. In contemplating the options outlined above the shareholder makes the following calculations.

Selling rights
The purchaser of the right could buy 125 shares at £1. In order to purchase the right from our shareholder the purchaser

calculates what is reasonable to pay, which is determined by the ex-rights share price.

The market values of the shares before the issue

= 500 000 at £1.35	= £675 000
Cash raised by the issue	
= 125 000 at £1	= £125 000
New market value of the company	£800 000
The new market price of the shares	= 800 000
	625 000
	= £1.28

The best the shareholder can expect is to sell the right to buy 125 shares for 28p per share, £35 in all. This means that our shareholder can gain £35 without changing the individual stake in the company. However, there is a reduction in the shareholder's percentage stake which currently represents 1% of the company (500 of 500 000), and will become 0.8% (500 of 625 000). Furthermore, the value of the shares held will fall from $500 \times 1.35 = £675$ to $500 \times 1.28 = £640$. That is, the value will fall by £35. Thus, selling the right neither makes nor loses the shareholder any money, but £35 worth of the original holding will have been sold.

Taking up full entitlement

No. of shares	Original value	New value	+/−
500	£675	£640	−£35
125	£125 (cost)	£160	+£35
625	£800	£800	−

The percentage of company shares held by the shareholder is maintained if he invests a further £125 in it. However, the gain to the shareholder of the discount price is cancelled out by the fall in the shares' market price.

Sell half the rights and take up half

Shareholder buys 63 shares at £1 each: cost, £63

Sale value of rights 62 × £0.28	=	£17.36
Market value of 563 shares ex-rights (£1.28)	=	£720.64
		£738.00
Total value of 500 shares cum rights (£1.35)	=	£675.00
Additional investment (63 × £1)	=	£63.00
		£738.00

The shareholder can increase his investment in the company but will neither gain nor lose any wealth.

Allowing rights to lapse

The effect on the shareholder's stake in the company would be to reduce it without gaining anything from selling rights to cancel the fall in value of the original holding. The Stock Exchange, however, requires companies making rights issues to sell any rights not taken up on behalf of the shareholders concerned, and distribute the profits to those shareholders, so they do receive some benefit from the issue.

Rights issues: share price effect

The calculations above have shown the theoretical effects of a rights issue on the share price. Theory and practice are, however, often different. The expectation may be to maintain or even increase the dividends after the issue but the share price may not be affected at all, in spite of the larger number of shares. The level of the ex-rights price, whether higher or lower than the theoretical level, depends to a large degree on the market's response to the issue and the proposals for the use of the funds. If the perception of the market is that the move is a good one then the share price is likely to fall only a little if at all, and thus the shareholder enjoys increased wealth. If, however, the proposals are seen in a poor light the price will fall more; if the issue is a small one, with the market not being flooded with new shares, the price will not drop very much.

Discounts and Underwriting

The calculations show that, when the market expects the company prospects to be unchanged by a rights issue, the wealth of shareholders remains unchanged. There is no transfer of wealth either between existing shareholders or to new shareholders. Underwriting in the issue of ordinary shares serves to ensure that the discount is reasonable and that the company will receive the funds it is trying to raise, even if the issue is a flop. The majority of rights issues are also underwritten, yet the calculations would suggest that the size of the discount is irrelevant. If the discount were set at 50% below the market price, then surely this would effectively guarantee the issue so that underwriting would no longer be necessary? In spite of this possible saving of underwriting fees, however, the so-called 'deep-discount' method is rarely used, though a notable deep-discount rights issue was made by Barclays Bank in 1985 when £22 million was saved in sub-underwriting fees.

The reasons for underwriting rights issues are twofold: the first is that many of the institutions who assume the underwriting risks are also major shareholders, particularly in the larger companies. While they may lose on the swings as shareholders by paying the underwriting fees, they gain on the roundabout of fees received as underwriters. The implication of this is, however, more significant than moving funds from one 'pocket' to another. Other shareholders, particularly individuals without investment in the underwriting institution, will lose by having to pay the underwriting fees without receiving any part of the fee in return. This view suggests that there may be some transfer of wealth from the non-institutional investor to those financial institutions holding shares.

The second, and perhaps more significant, purpose is to give a signal to the market. If an institution is prepared to take the risk of the issue being a failure, then this may affect the outlook of those considering their investment, and also enhance the market value of the company. This same argument casts doubt upon the wisdom of deep-discount issues because it suggests that the company is desperate for cash. Consequently, doubts are raised about company performance and value, and questions may be asked, such as, 'If the company prospects are so good, why does it need to offer such a deep discount?'

CONCLUSION

For the manager looking to raise finance for the company, the Stock Exchange offers a number of possibilities. However, the conditions of the Stock Exchange that must be met, while not particularly onerous, may represent a considerable change in the administration of the company's affairs. In addition, the issue of ordinary shares dilutes the managerial control of the company, perhaps not in the day-to-day running of the enterprise, but others will inevitably be involved in long-term planning. The company, after flotation, enjoys a much higher public profile and the associated pressures should be anticipated. Furthermore, the flotation itself may be a traumatic time for the company. However, Stock Exchange flotation is generally accepted as a natural progression for a successful enterprise and, in spite of the pressures, there are not many companies which, having gone through the process, wish to return to former arrangements.

CHAPTER FOUR

The markets for debt

Companies searching for finance must be aware of all the sources of funds. Debt capital is a major source of finance and is available from many providers. This chapter looks at the various approaches to debt finance open to managers.

Debt capital constitutes a third source of capital after equity capital and retained earnings (although, strictly speaking, retained earnings are equity capital). There are two fundamental types of debt capital: bank loan, and an issue of debentures. These types have a characteristic in common in that they both require the company to pay fixed interest. While the calculation of the interest payable on the bank loan or on debenture stock is straightforward, the determination of the cost of debt capital is complex.

BANK LOANS

It was not until 1979 that the clearing banks began making loans with a maturity term in excess of ten years. In the case of a loan to smaller companies the fixed interest rates are normally set at a premium over base rate (typically a premium of 3%–6%). Larger companies with a good credit rating are generally offered the premium on the inter-bank rate which is lower than the base rate. Loans are normally secured on personal guarantee by the directors or owners of small companies, and, in the case of larger companies, a charge is made against the assets of the company. If the charges are 'fixed' they are linked with a specific asset. 'Floating' charges are made on the assets generally. The costs of a bank loan consist of three main elements.

1. Interest rate. As well as the calculation outlined above, in some cases there may be an additional charge in the form of an 'arrangement fee' or 'negotiation fee'. This fee is usually in the region of 1% of the loan.
2. Security. The security demanded by the bank may be quite varied, but most term loans are secured. Secured loans are the most common, but there are others. It should be noted that a company may be able to take advantage of the government's Loan Guarantee Scheme, where the company is not required to provide security. When security is required the bank may restrict the company's right to issue other debt, or to sell assets, or even to pay dividends. The dangers involved in high gearing levels are outside the scope of this chapter, but in cases where the company's operations go seriously wrong banks have been forced to reschedule debts. However, this is not an easy decision for the banks to make. If they insist upon the terms of the covenants it may force the company out of business altogether in order to meet the repayments. Restructuring also involves a risk, often resulting in the banks allowing the firm to sell assets on which a charge has been made, in order to raise working capital to reinvest in the company.
3. Repayments. Term loans are relatively easy to arrange and repayment is usually through systematic amortization payments made over the full life of the obligation, but this is not a rigid rule. Repayment schedules are open to individual arrangements between bank and borrower. Sometimes banks allow a 'holiday' or 'grace' period before the borrower has to start repaying the loan. This is to enable the firms to become firmly established and to generate a sufficiently healthy cash flow.

In considering an application for a loan the bank may decide to impose some restrictions upon the financial operations of the borrower. Such restrictions might include a set ratio of current assets to current liabilities. Banks may also require the company to provide them with regular financial forecasts and statements.

The banks' decision to offer term loans, especially at variable interest rates, has been greeted enthusiastically by companies, and many use bank loans as a major source of debt capital.

In essence, the term loan is a long-term debt. Such loans are available not only from banks but also from equipment manufacturers and insurance companies. Almost every kind of business uses this type of debt, and term loans are especially important to small firms which face particular difficulties in raising finance (see 'Problems faced by small firms' below). However, companies actually like term loans for a number of reasons.

1. Term loans usually offer competitive rates, and can be arranged relatively easily and quickly. This type of arrangement has the added advantage of convenience.
2. The formal procedures, when compared with the requirements for a full listing on the Stock Exchange, for example, are minimal.
3. The key provisions of the debt are usually worked out more quickly and with much greater flexibility than is normally the case with public issues.
4. The term to maturity is also flexible, depending upon the size of the loan. The period can be from a minimum of three years to a maximum of seven to ten years, although longer maturities are not impossible.
5. The loan is usually retired through systematic amortization made over the full life of the loan. The availability of a negotiated flexible repayment schedule clearly makes these loans particularly attractive to companies which expect cash-flow surges.

OTHER LOANS

Loans are available from other financial institutions. However, companies tend to be reluctant to use these sources as interest payments are fixed. Should inflation fall, then borrowing at fixed rates could prove expensive. Sources of loans, in addition to the clearing banks, include pension funds, insurance companies (which occasionally make loans over 20 years), merchant banks, and the European Investment Bank. Furthermore, there are specialist financial institutions such as the Industrial and Commercial Finance Corporation (ICFC) which is part of the giant Investors in Industry (3i).

Mention should be made of the medium term note. This is another category of security that enables company treasurers to have a wide range of options. A medium term note is a promissory note, written by the company, promising to pay a specified amount on a specified date. The procedure is for the company to write the note and then to sell it in the marketplace. The interest rate may fluctuate or may be fixed, and the maturity date can be anything from something less than a year to as long as fifteen years.

PROBLEMS FACED BY SMALL FIRMS

Small firms face particular difficulties in raising finance. There are a number of characteristics shared by smaller companies which make it difficult for them to obtain funds, which include the following.

1. The shorter trading record of small companies means that less is known of them.
2. The smaller the company the less likely it is to enjoy the accounting skills which are required to put over a strong case for financing.
3. Access to markets for securities, in particular the Stock Exchange, is difficult and expensive.

4. It is always difficult to obtain venture capital, though smaller firms are often in need of it.
5. Smaller companies are less able to diversify, and thus may be at greater risk.
6. It is a widely held view that smaller companies are more likely to face liquidation, and thus potential lenders will be harder to persuade.
7. The market for finance is largely dominated by the institutions, which in itself causes problems for the small company. Financial institutions usually seek to invest in such a way as to ensure that their particular investment is unlikely to affect share prices, and thus the strategy is to invest small amounts in larger companies. Furthermore, the institutions require, or rather prefer, stable long-term growth, and they are unlikely to find this in small companies.
8. There are substantial transaction costs involved in raising finance. Some of these costs are fixed, and thus the raising of a relatively small sum for a smaller company leads to higher relative costs.

The combined effect of these problems is that small firms are more or less dependent on banks for finance. Institutions that invest in smaller companies will perceive a higher level of risk; as a consequence, the expected returns are higher and the cost of capital is thus raised.

DEBENTURES

A debenture is a document issued in return for money lent. There are various types of debenture but they have some features in common. They are usually in the form of a bond undertaking the repayment of the loan on a specified date, and with regular stated payments of interest between the date of issue and the date of maturity. These payments of interest are to be paid before a dividend is paid to *any* class of share holder. The Companies Acts define the word 'debenture' as including debenture stock and bonds. Often the expressions 'debenture' and 'bond' are interchanged, and the term 'loan stock' can also be used. As a general guide, the word debenture is used to refer to secured issue, and 'loan stock' is used to describe the less secure issues. It is important to note here that debentures can only be offered to the public when the issue is accompanied by a prospectus.

A mortgage debenture is secured. That is to say, a particular real asset of the company has a charge placed upon it, which means that the creditors have security. The principal drawback is associated with the restrictions on proposals to dispose of assets on which a charge is made. These may be quite inflexible in the sense that the company cannot dispose of them while there is a charge upon them, although this is not always the case.

Debentures with a floating charge indicate that the charge, giving security to the creditor, is levied upon all the assets of the company. This cannot be applied to assets which already have a mortgage debenture charged on them, of course, but other assets may be used. This type allows a greater flexibility in the use and disposal of assets by the company. If the company were to mismanage the debenture and fail to pay the interest, then the debenture holders, with court approval, may appoint a receiver to administer the company assets until the interest has been paid up in full.

Some debentures are unsecured, and the creditors in this instance have no security. All they have is the company's note of indebtedness. Should the company assets be liquidated, then holders of unsecured debentures will not be paid until the holders of secured debentures have been paid.

Convertible debentures may be changed, at the decision of the holder (but only in specific conditions), into a designated number of ordinary shares in the company. The most significant special feature of convertible debentures is the conversion ratio which dictates the number of shares to be received when the security is given up, that is to say, on conversion. Linked with this ratio are other terms.

(a) The conversion price is the price at which debenture stock may be converted to shares. The conversion price is always at a figure above the market price of the shares at the time of issuing the stock.

(b) The conversion ratio states the number of shares to which each £100 of debenture stock may be converted. This is basically an alternative way of expressing the conversion price.

Example £250 000 of 10% convertible loan stock has been issued at par value. The terms for conversion are that £10 of stock may be converted to six £1 shares. The conversion price is:

$$£10 \div 6 = £1.67$$

Thus the par value of stock required to obtain a single ordinary share is £1.67. The conversion ratio is calculated as follows:

$$\frac{6 \div 10}{£1} = 0.60$$

This indicates that for every £1 of stock that is converted, 0.60 shares are obtainable.

The conversion premium demonstrates by how much the current share price would have to rise in order to match the conversion price. Thus, if at the date of issue the current share price is set at 80p and the conversion price is set at £1, then the conversion premium is 25%. If at the date of conversion the share price has risen by more than 25%, the stockholder will be able to convert into shares and then sell them at the higher figure, thus realizing capital gain. Due to this potential for gain, convertible debentures are usually issued at a lower rate of interest than other loan stock. The possibility of making this capital gain is strongly influenced by the conversion premium. If the premium was set very high, then the likelihood is that the gain would be small, so the interest offered would need to be that much higher in order to make the issue attractive.

On the assumption that the conversion rate is correctly set, the convertible has two particular advantages for the company. The first is that as earnings continue to grow the loan becomes self-liquidating. That is, as the company enjoys increased earnings, share prices reflect the situation by rising in price. The share price will soon reach a price at which conversion is worthwhile, and at this point the debentures are exchanged for existing shares. The conversion of bonds to shares actually helps the company because it no longer needs to be concerned with raising finance to service the debt. Existing shareholders do not enjoy the benefits of conversion. The net effect of conversion from their point of view is that their holding is diluted, and when asked, would probably promote the idea of raising new debt to pay off the old loan. The second advantage of convertibles enjoyed by the company is that conversion does not harm the capital structure of the company. Issue of loan stock requires the payment of interest but the capital does not have to be repaid directly. Conversion does not increase the amount of capital employed. The conversion process obviously reduces the gearing of the company and this, in itself, may enable a new round of debt financing without overstepping any debt ratio limitations.

A class of debenture that is not often issued is that known as the irredeemable debenture, though the name is a little misleading in that the company does have the option to redeem. As with other debentures, the company may purchase the irredeemable debentures from the holder with the holder's agreement, or as they come on the market. An irredeemable debenture does not have a maturity date on which the holder can claim redemption. These are not very popular with lenders: the company may, if both parties agree, redeem the debenture, but the lender cannot demand payment. In selecting the time for redemption, the company has to exercise caution. The main factor will be that of minimizing the costs associated with the operation, such as the costs of refinancing the debt and the actual costs of the redemption process. Samuels, Wilkes, and Brayshaw (1990) suggest that a better name might be 'perpetual' rather than irredeemable.

There are a number of reasons why an investor would

choose debentures in preference to other forms of company financing. The first is to do with risk. Debt financing usually has a fixed maturity. The investor enjoys priority in both interest and in the event of the company going into liquidation. In addition, debenture holders receive a fixed return on the investment: should the company fail to make large profits, the debenture holders are paid at the fixed interest rate while ordinary shareholders, for example, must await the board's decision on whether or not, and at what level, to pay dividends. All is not to the benefit of the debenture holder, however. The fixed interest rate, say 6%, may be attractive in giving some security, but if the debenture is held over, say, 20 years, and there has been significant inflation over the period, then the 6 pence in the £1 has been seriously eroded in its real value. Debenture holders do not have voting rights, which restricts their control as long as the company is solvent; should it go into liquidation, however, it is the debenture holders who will, in effect, take control.

There are both advantages and disadvantages for the investee in issuing debentures. The primary advantages include the fact that the cost of the debt is known and is limited. If the company makes greater profits, these are not shared out with the debenture holders. The cost of the debt is also limited because the risk to debenture holders is lower than for shareholders. Furthermore, existing shareholders do not find that their control of the company is diluted due to a debenture issue, and neither are they asked to supply the additional finance the company is looking for. Finally, the interest payment that is made to the debenture holder is a deductible payment for tax purposes.

However, from the company point of view, debenture issues are not an unqualified benefit. There is a greater risk to the company due to debt financing if the company does not perform as well as expected. Where the returns made to shareholders may be reduced in line with reduced profits, the debenture debt is fixed, the interest must be paid, the charges are fixed. Debentures, by and large, have a fixed maturity date, and the company must make preparations to repay the debt on maturity. The expectations and plans which initially called for the debt financing to be arranged may change over the life of the debt. In the best circumstances long-term debt can be advantageous, but the converse is also true. Assumptions that were made ten years ago about the future trading position of the company, for example, may prove to be erroneous and the decisions for long-term debt unwise. Companies cannot raise an unlimited amount of funds from debt financing. The standards of financial policy which have general acceptance dictate acceptable debt ratio limits which must not be exceeded.

On entering agreements for debt financing, the orthodox practice is for the parties to enter into a loan agreement. This document, which must be signed by the borrower, should include a number of provisions, ranging from the repayment schedule and possible 'prepayment' terms and interest charges, to whether a commitment fee is payable by the borrower, what information the borrower must give the lender over the period of the loan, and any negative covenants the borrower may impose.

Negative covenants restrict certain rights of the borrower until the debt controlled by the covenants has been repaid in full. Measures imposed in such covenants often include one or more of the following:

(a) restrictions on raising the level of debt supported by the borrower;
(b) disposal of certain assets may be disallowed;
(c) unless already allowed as part of the loan agreement there may be restriction upon the payment of cash dividends, share redemption, and issues of options;
(d) the ratio of annual cash flow to annual interest and repayment charges may have to be maintained at a specified level.

The rationale for negative covenants is the protection of the lender. While they cannot offer protection if the company should default, they can wield influence over situations which otherwise may increase the risk of default. The lender's risk can be further reduced by employing some damage control techniques known as credit enhancements. Included in this category are credit insurance, guarantees from a third party, and collateral.

WARRANTS

The holder of a warrant is entitled to purchase a precise number of shares at a specified price on a particular date. Thus a warrant is, in principle though not exactly, a call option issued by the company on its own stock. The main difference is that when the warrant is exercised the company issues new treasury stock in return for the exercise price specified in the contract, whereas a call option allows the writer to supply the holder with stock that has already been issued. Warrants have no voting rights, do not pay interest, and offer no claim on the assets of the company. One of the most common ways of warrant issue is as an encouragement to investors in debentures – that is, they are used to make the offer more attractive. There have been instances where warrants have been offered to employees when their company has merged. They have also been successfully employed as compensation for underwriters and venture capitalists. Where warrants are linked to a bond or debenture issue it is possible to detach them and trade them separately, and these are known as 'detachable' warrants.

As with convertibles, there are certain advantages to the company issuing warrants. Warrants enable the company to maintain the loan stock until the date of redemption as well as allowing the company to issue new capital, because the conversion of one form of financing to another does not apply.

The problems that face a young company without a proven track record in raising finance have already been outlined above. An investor may be cautious in taking debenture stock because of the difficulties in assessing the risk of default, and as a consequence investors may demand a high interest rate in order to compensate for the risk. Debenture holders have no option to benefit from the company performing well, and thus it is that companies may be able to tempt investors to their debenture stock if the pill is sweetened by the issue of some convertibles or warrants, in return for lower interest rates in the immediate term.

If a company performs poorly and the value of its stock falls, there may be a conflict of interests between shareholders and bondholders. Shareholders may encourage the management to take risks, with the idea that they have nothing to lose but everything to gain. Debenture holders, on the other hand, who may hold debentures with the company assets as security, may hold a different view, because they could not participate in any possible upside gain as a result of a new project. They will not encourage the management in ventures which could make or break the company. However, they may be tempted if they are given the opportunity to share in future possible upside gains through the issue of warrants or convertibles. It is for these reasons that the most common issuers of warrants and convertibles are risky companies, young companies, or those companies whose risk profile is difficult to estimate.

OTHER BONDS

The bond market has become more flexible through the introduction of a variety of bonds with what may be described as atypical characteristics.

Drop lock bonds attempt to make a link between a floating rate loan and a long-term, fixed-interest stock. It is a type of Local Authority bond which generally enjoys a flexible interest rate. The rate used is linked directly to prevailing short-term interest rates. Drop lock bonds vary from this pattern in one respect: in order to protect the investor against excessive falls in interest rates there is a level, set in advance, below which the interest paid on the bonds is not allowed to fall.

A form of raising finance that has become more common in recent years is the deep-discounted bond. The term 'discounted' in this case refers to the difference between the price at which the security is issued and the amount that is payable on redemption. The calculation excludes all the interest that is to be paid on the bond while it is in issue. The clear attraction of the deep-discounted bond to the investor is that the redemption yield can be extremely high. In order to qualify for the description 'deep', the discount offered has to be in excess of 15% of the amount payable at redemption.

Another type of bond which offers no interest during the lifetime of the issue but offers capital gain on redemption is the zero coupon bond. The advantage to companies is that no payments are required until the end of the life of the bond. This can be a great help for a company with short-term cash-flow difficulties. The prospective investor needs to have some guide as to whether the investment offers competitive rates of return. The following formula calculates the redemption yield of the bond:

$$Pt = \frac{I}{(1+r)} + \frac{I}{(1+r)^2} + \ldots + \frac{R}{(1+r)^n}$$

where Pt = current security market price
R = redemption value
I = annual interest payment
r = redemption yield
n = number of years to redemption

From this formula the yield of the following proposition can be calculated. A company has decided to issue a zero coupon bond in 1991 priced at £100. The bond will be redeemable in ten years at a price of £200. The redemption yield (r) can be calculated from the formula above:

$$£100 = \frac{£200}{(1 + r)^{10}}$$

Therefore the annual redemption yield is 7%. The investor's decision will be based upon whether the 7% offered by the bond compares favourably with other available forms of investment with similar risk profiles.

There is a further section of the bond market which concerns the issue of stock by the Government. As well as raising money for the government, stock issues by the government provide a relatively safe investment. For example, index-linked government stock, as its name suggests, has interest rates linked to the retail price index and thus protects investments against the effects of inflation. The consequence of this 'safety' is that the interest rates offered are low. The first issue of this stock, designed to help institutions with long-term investment commitments, such as pension funds and life assurance companies, offered 2% interest.

Investors may well desire to protect their investment from the ravages of interest rate changes, known as interest rate hedging. In January 1981 the government entered the fray by issuing 12% Exchequer Stock 1985, which was a means of hedging against future rates of interest. At six-monthly intervals from September 1981 to September 1983 the stock was convertible to 13.5% Exchequer Stock 1992 at a reducing percentage per £100 of the conversion. Thus the conversion rate in September 1981 was 99% of the 13.5%. The rate was reduced progressively every six months so that by September 1983 the rate was down to 92% of the 13.5%.

Other low-risk investment opportunities from the government, gilt-edged securities, compete with company securities on the Stock Exchange. Debentures and equities both offer returns above those offered by gilts. In the case of debentures, the difference is usually 1%, while equities, because of the associated risk, offer a little more. The system runs into difficulties in times of inflation, when government gilts give a higher return than equities due to investors selling their fixed interest securities and buying shares which are not fixed, and thus are not affected so detrimentally by the effects of inflation. This situation is known as the 'reverse yield gap'.

Particularly high interest rates were experienced during the early seventies, and reached a peak in 1975. The annual figures produced by the Central Statistical Office demonstrated an interesting correlation between interest rates and the issue of particular instruments for raising finance. The issue of debentures during the seventies fell. This was as expected, reflecting the higher rates that companies had to pay to secure new loans. The issues of convertible debentures increased after 1967 as the levels of inflation rose, whereas after 1969 the level of convertible issues fell. This pattern does not follow the course of inflation rates directly, but is probably an indication of the weak state of the stock market in the early seventies. After 1975 the issues of convertible debentures grew again. The evidence suggests that, during a period of increasing difficulty in forecasting the rate of inflation and interest rate patterns, there was a substantial move by business to use hybrid forms of financing. While there may not be a direct correlation between interest rates and stock issues, the former wield considerable influence over the means companies will use as sources of finance in the long term.

Mezzanine debt and junk bonds

Mezzanine debt is used by a company to finance leveraged takeovers, company restructuring, or management buyouts. Its name refers to its position somewhere between equity shares (it is not as risky) and the secured debt of a company (demanding a lower level of security). The term 'mezzanine finance' is applied in the USA to preference shares, convertible loans, and loans which are subordinate to the secured debt. Mezzanine debt tends to be used by companies which are not well established, and thus is seen as high-risk/high-yield finance.

In order for smaller companies to take over larger companies, 'junk bonds' may be used. The cash is raised by the bond issue and the intention is to sell the assets of the larger company in order to repay the debt. The junk bond market has not become established in the UK.

Preference shares

Holders of preference shares are part owners of the company, but preference shares are closer to loan capital than to ordinary shares. Although in the payout pecking order preference shares rank below debentures, they are above ordinary shares.

However, the greatest similarity is that they attract a fixed rate of dividend While the dividend does not have to be paid in the current year, the shares tend to be cumulative and arrears from previous years have to be paid before the current year's dividends are paid to ordinary shareholders. Some preference shares are not cumulative, however. An additional feature is that 'participating preference shares' are entitled to a share in remaining profits after the fixed dividend has been paid. The shares cannot usually be redeemed, the shareholder disposing of the holding through the stock market. The advantage to the company is that the preference shares are a source of long-term, though not permanent, finance. A clear company advantage is the fact that the dividend does not have to be paid if profits do not justify it, and the dividend is not as high as for ordinary shares. Holders of preference shares do not have voting rights, so an issue of preference shares does not dilute the current shareholders' position. If they are redeemable, then they must be considered as debt when calculating the level of gearing of the company, but the dividends paid are not tax deductible. Preference shares are not really popular with companies or investors, and issues are quite rare. In 1993 only 7.7% of the total.

THE COST OF DEBT CAPITAL

Companies may issue both debentures and preference shares with the right for the holder to convert them to ordinary shares under specific terms and conditions. When such a right is offered, the company pays a lower dividend while the stock is unconverted; on conversion, it does not have to raise the cash to redeem the debt, but instead issues new ordinary shares in exchange. The investment of the original funds should be enough to cover the costs of the conversion.

Debenture holders are entitled to receive interest payments from the company. If the debentures are 'irredeemable' or 'perpetual' the interest payments will continue throughout the life of the holder, or until the company chooses to redeem them. If the debentures are redeemable then interest payments are due until the company pays the final redemption, which will be the face value of the debt.

The cost to the holder of a debenture depends on the circumstances under which it was bought. Debentures purchased at the time of issue may result in the purchaser being able to take advantage of a discount on the market value. In the case of debentures bought in the secondary market, then clearly the purchaser's cost is the market value of the debenture. In considering the cost of capital the market value is the most relevant measure of the two, because the market value represents the present value of a stream of cash flows that the holder will receive. The cost of the issued debt capital is equal to the discount rate required to equate the cash flow stream and the market value.

The company manager may use the following formula to calculate the cost of capital for debentures which are irredeemable.

$$Kd = \frac{i}{Do}$$

where Kd = the cost of debt capital

i = interest paid

Do = the market price of debt capital after payment of current interest

The interest paid to debenture holders, often referred to as the 'coupon', is usually included in the name of the debenture. For example, a '10% debenture' shows that for every £100 of face value of the debenture £10 or 10% is paid in interest. Therefore, the actual cash amount due to the holder is determined by the relationship between the stated interest rate to the face value of the bond. The face value could well be different from the market value, which will fluctuate with variations in interest rates. This, of course, applies to the fixed-rate debenture.

Taking the above example, 10% irredeemable debentures, with a market value of £95 and interest due to be paid in one year's time, will have a cost of debt equalling the interest rate (10%) divided by the market price (£95) multiplied by 100 = 0.1052 or 10.5%.

The calculation for redeemable debentures is different. Suppose the debentures were issued as 9% debentures with a market value of £92, redeemable in five years' time with a redemption value of £96. The calculation must cater for the fact that the present market value of £92 will be equal to the discounted present value of future receipts (£9 per year for five years followed by a repayment of £96).

The first step is to identify the interest rate which will discount the cash flows (years 1–5, £9: year 5, £96) to equality with the current market value (£92). This requires a discount factor (IRR) which will result in a net present value (NPV) of zero for the cash flows, which are:

Year 0	£ (92)
Year 1	£ 9
Year 2	£ 9
Year 3	£ 9
Year 4	£ 9
Year 5	£ 9
Year 5	£ 96

Interpolation is used, thus:

$$92 = \underset{t1}{\frac{9}{(1 + r)}} + \underset{t2}{\frac{9}{(1 + r)^2}} + \underset{t3}{\frac{9}{(1 + r)^3}} + \underset{t4}{\frac{9}{(1 + r)^4}} + \underset{t5}{\frac{9 + 96}{(1 + r)^5}}$$

$$0 = -92 + 9 \sum_{t = 1}^{t = 5} dfr + 96dfr$$

where r = the internal rate of return
df = discount factor for the IRR in year t

In the formula above using 10%:

$$NPV = -92 + (3.79 \times 9) + (96 \times 0.621)$$
$$= -92 + 34.11 + 59.6$$
$$= 1.71$$

Whereas using 11%:

$$NPV = -92 + (3.69 \times 9) + (96 \times 0.593)$$
$$= -92 + 33.21 + 59.6$$
$$= -1.89$$

Thus, via interpolation, the IRR is approximately 10.5%

TAXATION AND THE COST OF DEBT CAPITAL

Whether a company has borrowed from a bank or debenture holder the interest due must be paid. Taxation has a substantial effect on the cost of the debt. Because the interest paid to the investor is allowable for tax as a business expense, the cost to the company is not the full agreed interest rate. This is best demonstrated by an example of two companies EquiCo plc and DebenCo plc. They have both made the same pre-tax profits. EquiCo plc is financed by equity and DebenCo plc by debt capital. The following table shows the significant difference to after-tax profits because of the type of finance used.

	EquiCo plc £	DebenCo plc £
Pre-tax profits	110 000	110 000
Interest payable	–	11 000
	110 000	99 000
Corporation Tax @ 25%	27 500	24 750
Profits after tax	82 500	74 250

Note that DebenCo plc has a tax advantage which can offset some of the interest cost. However, any tax advantage accruing due to debt capital would be nullified in periods of high interest rates. In addition, the equity-financed company would have further disbursements of dividend payments. Furthermore, debt capital only produces advantages in tax terms to profitable companies. If a company was not in a tax-paying position then it would gain nothing from using debt capital.

Finally, the formula below expresses the effect taxation has on the cost of debt capital.

$$Kd = \frac{i}{Do} (1-t)$$

where Kd = cost of debt capital (taking taxation into account)

Do = market price of debt capital after payment of current interest

t = applicable taxation rate

i = coupon

When compared with other forms of finance, debt capital tends to carry the lowest cost. Debt capital holders are taking lower risks due to the guarantee of a certain rate of interest, and preferential payment if the company should be liquidated, and they cannot therefore demand or expect as high a return as the more risky investments, such as equity. Furthermore, the fact that interest payments are tax deductible contributes to the relatively low cost of debenture capital.

LOAN CAPITAL

One of the main sources of finance for public companies is loan stock, and in fact, 45% of all the issues on the Stock Exchange in 1986 were of debt capital. The principal advantage of debt capital is that it is cheaper to issue and maintain than equity capital, coupled with the tax concessions associated with loan interest but not with dividends. Loan capital demands fixed, regular payments of interest and eventual repayment of the principal over a predetermined period. In order to raise funds in this way the company must be able to indicate that profits will be at a level to service the debt, and that assets are available as security to cover the repayments of principal and interest. Issues of loan stock also lead to the company creditors exercising effective control over the company, in order to protect their money. The degree to which this control is acceptable will help determine the level of loan stock to be issued.

VALUING A CONVERTIBLE LOAN STOCK

In order to calculate the value of a convertible it is vital to consider both its value as a straight bond and its conversion value. Clearly the straight bond value depends largely upon the interest rate, the date of maturity, and also the prevailing market interest rate on other bonds of similar risk. The straight bond value can be calculated using the following formula.

$$Bt = \sum_{t=1}^{t=m} \frac{C}{(1+i)^t} + \frac{M}{(1+i)^m}$$

where   Bt = value as a straight bond at time t
m = years to maturity
C = annual coupon payable on the bond
M = redemption value
i = market rate of interest for equivalent risk-class bonds

When there is adequate security for the bond and the firm is doing well then the value as a straight bond will not vary much with the firm value. However, should the risk of default increase, perhaps with the decline in the value of the firm, then the value of the bond may also decrease as a consequence.

There is additional value in the convertible stock due to the fact that it can be converted into shares. The conversion value is basically the market value of the bond if it were converted to shares *now*. The conversion value of a stock may be calculated by multiplying the conversion ratio by the current share price.

Example   Our investor holds £1000 of stock which is convertible at 50p, and is thus entitled to 2000 shares. If the shares are currently at 60p, then his conversion value of stock is 2000 × 60p = £1200 representing a gain on his investment of £200. If the value of shares had dropped to 30p, the conversion value of stock would be 2000 × 30p = £600. It may be that the convertible is worth more purely as loan stock; if so, the stockholder would not make the conversion.

The straight bond value and the conversion value provide two floors below which the value will never fall. The two values may be combined to give the effective floor price for a specific firm value.

There will be a difference in the value of the loan stock at the time of conversion and its value when issued. This difference is known as the conversion premium, and is normally shown as a percentage of the conversion value. Companies will aim for the highest possible conversion premium because it reduces the number of shares that have to be issued to complete the conversion.

LEASING

As an alternative to borrowing, the economic value of leasing is calculated by discounting the incremental cash flows of the lease over the borrowing alternative. In addition, there are taxation benefits, leasing helps to preserve cash, and it varies the borrowing portfolio. Furthermore, leasing tends to be a less restrictive source of finance. The main attraction is the certainty and flexibility that allows company executives to reduce risk, thus allowing more precise expense budgeting; as such, it has great appeal to small businesses. The leasing contract also has a number of advantages in the areas of planning and administration. Within the planning function the cash flows are smoothed by the use of contract leasing because relatively small regular payments are spread over a long period, whereas purchase of an asset would result in a single lump-sum payment. Certainty is enhanced because leasing contracts cannot be cancelled, compared with a bank overdraft facility which can be withdrawn. There is greater flexibility because the leasing contract can be tailored to suit individual company needs. Because a lease allows the immediate use of an asset there is also a degree to which it is a hedge against inflation.

Administrative advantages include the convenience of the arrangement, as leases are usually quicker and easier to arrange than other debt and equity arrangements. Because rentals are operating expenses, management in divisionalized companies will enjoy greater freedom in their investment decision process. Leasing also presents a much easier book-keeping procedure due to the fixed and regular nature of rental payments compared with the range of payments for purchase, insurance, and maintenance which are involved in the purchase of an asset.

CONCLUSION

As a major source of finance, debt capital and its distinguishing features are commonly experienced by managers. The distinguishing features of debt capital are (a) it is less expensive than equity capital; (b) because it is a lower-risk investment the investor is happy with a lower rate of return; and (c) interest payments, as an expense whether or not profit is made, are tax deductible.

REFERENCE

Samuels, J.M., Wilkes, F.M., and Brayshaw, R.E. (1990) *Management of Company Finance* 5th edn, Chapman & Hall, London, p. 239.

CHAPTER FIVE

Eurocurrency markets

WHAT IS A EUROCURRENCY MARKET?

It is in the nature of the business of financial institutions, seeking depositors and borrowers, to make arrangements for loans in a foreign country. A US depositor, for example, may wish to make a dollar deposit in the London office of a financial institution. In addition, a company with considerable activity in France may wish to borrow sterling from the same institution's Paris office. The significant part of these transactions is that the currency involved is being dealt with in a country other than its own. In these circumstances a Eurocurrency market is said to exist.

The most important Eurocurrency markets are the Eurodollar, Euromark, and Eurosterling. The UK exporter looking for funds will discover that the Eurocurrency and Eurobond are major sources of finance. Essentially, the Eurocurrency market is an inter-bank activity of enormous proportions, with the largest part being in overnight to three-months money.

The borrowing chain is easily linked up, for example:

US bank receives $ deposit
↓
US bank lends to a company
↓
Company deposits in another bank
↓
Second bank lends all or part

The Eurocurrency market is at the short- to medium-term end of the Euromarkets and is by far the largest of the international financial markets. Because Eurocurrency banking is not subject to many of the regulations and restrictions of domestic banking, it tends to be cheaper, more efficient, and more competitive. The Eurocurrency market operates only in currencies that are freely convertible into other currencies, such as the US dollar and the German mark, and only outside those currencies' country of origin. Eurobanks are therefore located in countries which do not regulate their foreign currency banking activities. There are, due to competition, close links between the national and Eurocurrency interest rates. A UK manufacturer may wish to borrow from a UK bank, or a Eurobank may be considered. The Eurobank will only be chosen if the rate of interest demanded is lower than or equal to that of a UK bank, which demonstrates how domestic interest rates effectively provide upper bounds for Eurobank rates.

The Eurocurrency markets are money markets rather than foreign exchange markets. Their importance in the context of international financial management is that they provide an alternative source of funds to domestic banks.

Eurocurrency loans are short- or medium-term loans. The term of a loan may be as long as five years, but most lending is for three months or less. There are a number of types of loan available.

1. Fixed-interest loans are usually over a medium term of up to five years, and the borrower knows in advance what the interest payments will be. However, interest rates are vulnerable and the variation in interest rates will limit the banks' willingness on amounts and duration of loans.
2. Stand-by credits are overdraft facilities offered by banks to customers in Eurocurrency. The cost of borrowing will be at an agreed rate in accordance with an agreed formula. The bank will also charge a commitment fee of 1% for funds which it has made available but which have not been drawn.
3. Most Eurocurrency loans are roll-over loans, where the bank agrees to make funds available over a given period of time,

say five years, but the interest rate is open to renegotiation every three or six months.

4. A number of banks may form themselves into a syndicate in order to provide a large loan to a single customer over a period that is longer than usual. Such loans are called syndicated loans.

A wide range of participants make use of the Eurocurrency markets. Most of the international corporations and banks which form the core of the borrowing customers are based in North America, Western Europe, or Japan. The institutions of the market consist of the commercial banks, which take part as both depositors and lenders, purchasing and issuing financial securities. The largest banks in the world are involved in the Eurodollar market, a Eurodollar being basically a US dollar which has been deposited with a bank outside the United States. It does not matter what the nationality of the bank is, it could be a branch of a US bank in a foreign country, or it could be a foreign bank. Although London may be regarded as the main centre for the Eurodollar market there are other important centres, including Paris, Frankfurt, Zurich, Nassau, Singapore, and Hong Kong (Singapore and Hong Kong deposits are called 'Asiadollars').

Non-bank participants are made up of firms dealing internationally: exporters, importers, and investors, as well as those with manufacturing operations across national frontiers. The attraction of the Euromarkets to these companies is that at times of tight credit at home Euromarket funds are always available, at a price. In such a large market as this the very size ensures that the marginal cost of funds is less.

The advantages to the borrower of using the Euromarket are that the lenders on the domestic market may discriminate, or larger sums may be required than are available in the home markets, or it may be deemed necessary to avoid the possibility of exchange control barriers.

There are four principal reasons why company managers should want to invest in a currency in an account outside its home country.

1. As a means of spreading risk. Some depositors have been unwilling to leave all their balances in a given currency in the same location and under the same jurisdiction. In the 1950s the Communist countries were afraid that the United States would try to sequestrate their dollar holdings. The US authorities have in the past frozen Iranian and Libyan assets. In the UK the high courts decided that is was not possible for the US authorities to freeze Eurodollar deposits in the London branch of a US bank.
2. Because the interest rate offered on the Eurodollar tends to be slightly higher than New York, the investor can earn more interest.
3. It is more convenient, when trading in Europe, to trade in the Eurodollar in Frankfurt or London, because if the company chose to trade in the domestic dollar, the market would be available for only half the working day.
4. Possible difficulties can be avoided. Occasionally, some European countries have made it difficult or impossible for foreigners to hold currencies within the country by the imposition of such measures as negative interest rates and exchange control barriers.

Companies will often wish to borrow in a foreign currency in order to obtain foreign exchange to finance overseas investment. Alternatively, the reason might be because of the difficulties experienced at particular times in obtaining credit and capital at home.

EUROBOND

The Eurobond market is much smaller than the Eurocurrency market, and in a fundamental sense performs the same function as the external money market. The Eurobond, most commonly issued in the US dollar, is one which is sold in a country other than the country of the issue. Thus, an American company would issue such a bond (dollar denominated) in the European markets. The funds for the market are gathered internationally, sorted into a variety of currencies, and then made available to borrowers of a variety of countries. The lending is not influenced or regulated by the national authorities of that currency, and dealers lend directly to borrowers on this market without the bank acting as intermediary. US borrowers began this market as a way of avoiding the stringent US interest rate regulations. For the system to function well it is dependent upon governments allowing movement of currency into and out of countries. Currently many of the borrowers in this market are public sector bodies or international organizations. Eurobonds are usually bearer-bonds rather than on a registered basis, which pay interest, at fixed or variable rates, on presentation of an interest coupon. Ownership is transferred by handing the bond itself to a new owner. Only companies that are listed on the Stock Exchange and who have issued a prospectus may issue Eurobonds. The interests of the bond holders is usually represented by a trustee, and paying agents are commonly appointed in various cities.

Eurobonds are clearly very different from Eurodollars. In the bond market the investor is able to hold the borrowers' securities directly. Eurodollars enable investors to hold claims in the short term on Eurobanks, while the banks hold the claim on the longer-term, more risky loans to the final borrowers. Like the Eurodollar market the Eurobond market is separate from the national markets and, to a degree, is not subject to the same restrictions and regulations as a national market.

There is some similarity between domestic bonds and Eurobonds in that they are claims on corporations or governments. However, there are also some characteristics which make them distinctive. National regulations on the issue of new bonds are avoided by the 'placing' of Eurobonds, and issued bonds are placed internationally at the same time with the multinational arms of the banks who can then sell them on throughout the world. The issue of Eurobonds is usually to countries other than the country of issue, and interest payable on Eurobonds is not subject to withholding tax. Domestic bonds held by non-residents usually have a withholding tax charged on them before interest is paid.

The issue of a Eurobond is managed in six principal stages.

1. The borrower needs to appoint a bank to manage the issue. This will most commonly be a merchant or an investment bank.
2. The bank the borrower has appointed then makes an approach to a number of other banks and institutions to help with the issue. This group is then known as the 'managing banks'.
3. The group of managing banks sets about inviting a number of banks and/or institutions to underwrite the issue.
4. The issue is then placed with a number of 'selling' banks.
5. The selling banks then try to place their allotment with their own clients. In order to facilitate this activity a prospectus will be prepared giving details of the issuer and the reasons for the issue.
6. In the UK a trust deed is usually used to constitute a Eurobond issue.

In the Euromarkets bond issues do not offer the same protection against over-gearing as the domestic market. The reassurance that is commonly given is that the new investors will not have greater security than existing bond holders. As a consequence of the sorts of risk faced in the Eurobond market, companies are often pressurized to issue bonds with covenants, the purpose of which is to state the minimum standards of interest cover the company will maintain. In addition, the company's maximum amount of leverage will be stated.

EURONOTES

Short-term Euronotes or European Commercial Paper (ECP) cover the short-term sector of the capital market, and the market is large. The note is created by a European company which agrees to pay the holder a specified sum on a particular date or dates. The note can be sold and traded.

Medium-term Euronotes are issued over terms ranging from

nine months to ten years, and bridge the gap between ECPs and the long-term bond market. This market has lower minimum requirements than the bond market and will lend to borrowers with a lower credit rating.

EURO-EQUITIES

The Euro-equity market, which peaked in 1987, has remained small. The market was opened in 1965 with issued bonds having an option to convert into equity. Subsequently it became possible, by means of an attached warrant which can be traded separately, to obtain equity without surrending the bond. The principal difficulty in achieving growth in the Euro-equity market is the lack of a large market for trading these equities which is independent of home stock markets. In order to make issues attractive to investors companies frequently offered 'sweeteners', which could include a rolling put option (see Chapter 9 for a full explanation). Whenever convertible preference shares were redeemed the yield would be equal to a predetermined fixed rate, say 9%. If there was a strong secondary market then Euro-equities may stay in Europe in preference to returning to home markets to trade.

EXPORT CREDITS GUARANTEE DEPARTMENT

As an exporter a company is subject to greater risks due to the risk of default, insolvency, and political and currency exchange. Companies are able to insure against loss on overseas investments through a scheme set up by the government in 1919 called the Export Credits Guarantee Department (ECGD). The scheme basically enables exporters to offer credit terms to buyers from other countries, without having to bear the credit through bank overdraft, for example. Thus the level of exporter's funds tied up in the sale is considerably reduced. Up to 80% of the export contract value is guaranteed under the scheme, and the government usually has the right of recourse. Since its inception it has played a progressively more important role in the loans made available through the clearing banks, many of which would not have been available without the work of the ECGD. The scheme is designed primarily for new investment and investment in developing countries. An application for insurance must be made before the investment is made.

When the business deal is a large one, over £250 000, an arrangement can be made whereby the exporting company receives payment immediately the goods are delivered or the contract has been completed satisfactorily. This is made possible by the ECGD guaranteeing a loan to the purchaser, an arrangement called the ECGD Buyer Credit Guarantee. The overseas purchaser is generally expected to pay the purchaser from their own resources from 15% to 20% of the contract price. The funds emanate from a UK bank, and are either made available by loan to the purchaser or to the purchaser's bank. Under these circumstances the exporter is able to carry out the deal free from risk. The borrowing agreement is between the UK bank and the purchaser, with the ECGD standing as guarantor.

Companies engaged in smaller deals can also benefit from similar credit arrangements, where the ECGD will open a line of credit through a UK bank to foreign governments, banks, or companies.

In addition it provides subsidized finance for medium-term credits. The government agrees a fixed rate of interest at which banks will provide the finance which is required, and the ECGD then reimburses the bank for the difference between the agreed fixed rate and the agreed commercial rate of return. Export credit finance is often required so that firms can limit their own exposure to loss and the banks can be sure of the security for their loans. At this stage it is important to note that the ECGD is not itself a source of finance. It does not offer loans but makes it easier for companies to secure loans from banks.

In order to cover the costs the ECGD insists on a spread of business, and will not allow a company to insure only the more dubious risks. In addition, there are further limits of exposure to particular countries and thus to political risk.

The guarantee for finance for exports on short-term credit is primarily the Comprehensive Bank Guarantee (bills and notes). This provides security for the exporter conducting business by means of bills or promissory notes for contracts on terms of less than two years. The Comprehensive Bank Guarantee (open account) provides security to the borrower selling on open account and cash against documents with credit up to 180 days.

When a company requires finance for exports sold on medium- and long-term supplier credit, and the existing cover is not sufficient to raise the funds, the ECGD provides the Specific Bank Guarantee. In order to have this made available the credit terms must be for two years or more and the payment secured by bills or notes. Other guarantees available include the Supplemented Extended Terms Guarantee and the Comprehensive Extended Terms Bank Guarantee which is available in respect of contracts providing up to five years' credit.

THE EUROPEAN INVESTMENT BANK (EIB)

The European Investment Bank, which is non-profit-making, does not seek depositors. The funds it raises are from subscriptions by the member states of the EC (each state agrees to subscribe a certain amount), in addition to borrowing on the international capital markets. It was set up in 1958 as a way of making loans available to public and private borrowers. The loans are made available with the object of developing the areas of the EC which are less developed than others, modernizing existing projects or developing fresh activities, and for supporting activities which generate interest across member states' boundaries.

Essentially, the EIB offers long- to medium-term loans in the currency of the borrower's choice (including ECUs), with terms of between seven and twelve years. The interest charged is reasonable, usually about 2% lower than the comparable UK bank rate. The risk associated with the venture does not result in higher interest charges, but the EIB requires a company to provide guarantees either from the home government or from a financial institution.

One of the major disadvantages of borrowing from the EIB is the stipulation that loans must be repaid in the currency in which they are borrowed. Movements in the values of currencies can cause substantial problems, and these were so great at one time that the UK Treasury offered a guarantee against exchange rate losses in return for a premium. However, this cover has not been available since 1984, because the Treasury suffered losses through the scheme.

At first the EIB used to be associated with large loans to large organizations, but many were critical of this position. In 1978, therefore, the EIB made available a large sum of money that could be used to finance small- and medium-scale industrial ventures, and would be earmarked for use by smaller to medium-sized firms. The operations of the EIB are mainly through agencies. Prospective borrowers apply to the agents, although larger applications are handled through a government. The level of funding provided is typically 50% of new fixed-asset investment, and is medium term. Loans from £15 000 to £50 000 were handled through the agents in 1988. The objectives of EIB loans through agents is to promote regional economic development and to help safeguard employment.

THE EUROPEAN MONETARY SYSTEM (EMS)

The aim of the EMS is to achieve closer monetary co-operation leading to a zone of monetary stability in Europe. It is hoped that the move to stability will lead to higher levels of intervention and fixed exchange rates. There are three main elements to the EMS.

The European Monetary Co-operation Fund (EMCF)

The EMCF is responsible for the administration of the exchange rate mechanism and the mechanisms used in intervention of the EMS. It is responsible also for the issue of ECUs to the central banks of the EMS in exchange for gold deposits, though gold does not actually change hands: they are notional deposits amounting to 20% of reserves.

The Exchange Rate Mechanism (ERM)

The Exchange Rate Mechanism (ERM) is the key element of the EMS. The ERM, by forcing participating countries to keep their currencies within agreed limits against one another, aims to create exchange rate stability. The European Currency Unit (ECU) is another aspect of the system, as are credit facilities and arrangements for the closer co-ordination of economic and monetary policies.

There are nine participating currencies:

Germany (deutschmark) Denmark (krone)
France (franc) Belgium/Luxembourg (franc)
Italy (lira) Ireland (punt)
Netherlands (guilder) Spain (peseta)
Portugal (escudo)

How the ERM works

Central rates Each ERM currency has a central rate against each of the other currencies in the scheme. When a currency joins the mechanism, or when there is a realignment, a central rate in relation to the ECU is given to each currency. This is used to establish the central rate against all the other participating countries. Changes cannot be made unilaterally, but must be made with the agreement of all the participating currencies.

Margins   Members of the ERM limit the exchange rate between their currency and other members' currencies. Seven of the nine currencies are allowed to fluctuate within margins up to 2.25% above or below their central rates. However, the United Kingdom and Spain allow wider margins, 6% either side of their central rates. The effective upper and lower limits are determined by the need for each currency to remain within the bands against all other ERM currencies simultaneously. Thus, the figure of 6% limits the sterling level to not more than 6% above the weakest currency or below the strongest currency.

Intervention   The central banks of participating countries are obliged to buy or sell at the limiting rates in order to prevent the currency moving beyond the set limits. This is effective because foreign currency dealers will know the rate at which they can purchase currency from the central banks and thus will not accept a lower price if selling, or a higher price if buying. In order to finance this sort of intervention there are credit facilities available to each country. The 'very short term facility' (VSTF) consists of each of the central banks automatically making unlimited credit available in its own currency, the use of the VSTF being overseen by the European Monetary Co-operation Fund. The EMCF also issues ECUs to the central banks in exchange for 20% of their gold and dollar reserves (ECU swaps). These ECUs have limited use, and may be used by the central banks (and certain other monetary institutions) for settling the debts between them arising out of the use of the VSTF, for example. All EMS members currently take part in the EMCF swap arrangements.

Realignments and the stability of the system: convergence Intervention through the VSTF is effective but only in the short term, and would not be sustainable without macro-economic policies in line with the agreed central rates. Throughout the

1980s the ERM has put pressure on monetary authorities to pursue convergent and low-inflationary policies. Although the system provides for changes in the central rates, any such realignments have to be agreed by all the ERM members and are used only as a last resort. There have been 12 realignments altogether since the EMS began in 1978, and realignment is less frequent now that ERM economies have converged and there have been reductions in inflation differentials.

The European currency unit (ECU)

The ECU is a 'basket' of community currencies and consists of specified amounts of each community currency. Relative amounts of each currency reflect the country's economic weight, and are normally reviewed every five years. All community currencies are included in the ECU basket. Individual currency conversion rates against the ECU can vary day by day depending on the movement of that currency in relation to other currencies within the ECU. The official ECU conversion rate is published daily. There are no ECU notes and coins, but it is possible to lend and borrow in ECUs. The borrowing company or government can then convert the ECUs into the currency required. The repayment, in this instance, would be in ECUs, which would involve further conversion.

The ECU has a number of functions, the principal of which are as follows.

(a) The ECU provides a means of comparing the valuations of member currencies.
(b) It allows a measure to be taken of any deviation from the norm of national currencies.
(c) It constitutes a unit of account which allows a means for companies to settle their debts (both companies being within the EC).
(d) Inter-state loans may also be settled using the ECU as a unit of currency.

Its function as a unit of currency makes the ECU very useful.

It allows banks from different member states to nominate the debts and claims between them, and also ensures that any exchange rate risks are shared between them, rather than falling upon only one party.

As has already been explained, the reserves of a participating member are held as ECUs. These may be used to repay official debts between the states, although not more than half of the debt may be repaid using ECUs.

As a unit of account, clearing banks can offer exporters the following ECU facilities: spot and forward foreign exchange, travellers' cheques, deposit loans, negotiable certificates of deposit, and a range of ECU-denominated money and capital market instruments. Samuels, Wilkes and Brayshaw (1990) describe the ECU as one of the 'success stories of the Community'. It could well be that, and eventually the ECU could be used as a currency in its own right.

CONCLUSION

Managers are required to make full use of the resources under their control. If a company has surplus cash, investment opportunities must be sought. When a company needs to raise money, then the money markets must be scrutinized for the most appropriate deal. Eurocurrency markets are among the areas of interest for company managers wishing to invest or raise finance.

While many of the operators in the Eurocurrency markets are larger banks and financial institutions, there are areas open to small and medium firms, and exporting companies can use the Eurocurrency markets' preferential rates of interest with the help of government guarantees. It is worth noting that there are plans to privatize the Export Credits Guarantee Department (COI, 1990); whether or not its role in the Eurocurrency markets will change significantly remains to be seen.

REFERENCES

Central Office of Information (1990) *Economic Briefing*, **1**, December, HM Treasury, London.

Samuels, J.M., Wilkes, F.M., and Brayshaw, R.E. (1990) *Management of Company Finance*, 5th Edition, Chapman & Hall, London.

CHAPTER SIX

The venture capital market

This chapter will look at the part played by the specialized venture capital market in providing investment capital to a variety of businesses. It will demonstrate why the market is rather different from other risk capital sources, and why it is needed. The development of the venture capital industry, and the different types of venture funds, will be examined. In conclusion, the advantages and disadvantages for managers using venture capital will be discussed.

WHAT IS VENTURE CAPITAL?

In essence, venture capital consists of funds invested in small, newly established enterprises in high-growth markets which promise exceptional future profit levels. The investment is normally made in the form of equity capital, although some venture capital funds invest a mixture of equity and debt finance in these enterprises.

As the venture capital industry has grown, and venture capital funds have provided finance to meet the needs of a wider range of businesses than only those in start-up situations, so it has become more difficult to give a precise definition of 'venture capital'. Many funds now provide finance for management buy-outs, and to businesses for expansion purposes. Not even the British Venture Capital Association offers an overall definition of venture capital. Instead, membership of the Association is open to any institution which is 'active in managing funds for long-term equity investment in British unlisted companies'.

Shilson's definition (1984) highlights the three characteristics which most distinguish venture capital funding from other types of investment. According to Shilson, venture capital is: 'a way in which investors support *entrepreneurial talent* with finance and *business skills* to exploit market opportunities and thus to obtain *long-term capital gain'*. (Emphasis added)

It is this 'hands-on' approach of venture capital funds, providing managerial skills and general business support to the enterprises in which they invest, which allows venture capitalists to finance such high-risk projects.

The definition further suggests that the investor will obtain long-term capital gains. From this it is clear that the investments are in developing companies and are coupled with the venture capitalists wanting to achieve optimum returns from their investment. Venture capitalists are also prepared to wait for the optimum time, which is usually around five to seven years, or perhaps longer, so the investment is definitely long term. In looking for capital gains from the investment, venture capitalists do not generally take dividends or interest payments. This is because with a developing company, taking annual payments will mean less funds available to the company to expand and become more profitable; since the venture capitalists want optimum returns it is in their best interests not to take funds away at a most critical time for a company. The venture capitalists thus allow the company to expand and become as profitable as possible, which in turn increases the value of the venture capitalist's investment.

WHY THE VENTURE CAPITAL MARKET IS NEEDED

One of the reasons entrepreneurs find it difficult to raise investment finance from traditional external sources is because the business is not well established. Indeed, the company may be looking for start-up or early-stage growth financing, which means that potential investors have little information on which to judge the viability of a project (such as profit and loss accounts and historic earnings per share ratios); in addition, they often cannot judge how good the management team is because there is no track record. This lack of information means that any investment becomes very risky, and this risk increases the longer the funding period.

Consequently, if funding could only be obtained from the usual arm's-length financing methods (such as through the stock markets), most new projects and businesses would not receive the long-term capital funding they need.

What makes it possible for venture capitalists to invest in such long-term projects which are untried, unknown, and high risk? They can make their investments because they take a far more active approach in order to reduce the risk of their investments than do the passive investors of the stock market. The viability and the potential of the business, as well as the ability and experience of the management team, are investigated thoroughly in what is called the 'due diligence' process. This helps to reduce the information gap between the investor and the investee company and, therefore, the degree of risk to the investor.

The venture capitalist remains involved with the management of the business after the investment has been made, if such an approach is required. This managerial/advisory role used to be *de rigueur* for the venture capitalist, but has become less so recently, as venture funds have diversified into financing management buy-outs and other later-stage funding. In these cases the management team is sufficiently experienced to have little need of such help.

THE DEVELOPMENT OF THE VENTURE CAPITAL MARKET

The industry in its present form is based upon United States practice, but according to Lorenz (1985) venture capital can be traced back to the fifteenth century when merchant venturers went on voyages to establish businesses in different parts of the world. The funding for such expeditions came from wealthy individuals who did not journey themselves but left the risks to the entrepreneurs.

Venture capital in the form we know it today started to evolve around the late eighteenth and early nineteenth century. At this time entrepreneurs were emerging who were looking for wealthy individuals to invest in their projects. By the mid-nineteenth century the process had become more formalized when companies were set up to build railways in parts of South America and the growing British Empire, among other high-risk projects.

As early as 1931 the MacMillan Committee Report identified the existence of a 'finance gap' for small firms and businesses. At that time the Charterhouse Development Fund was set up specifically to provide new and growing ventures with risk capital. Another early venture fund was the Industrial and Commercial Finance Corporation, which was established at the end of the Second World War and is now part of the giant Investors in Industry (3i) plc.

It was not until the 1980s that the industry really took off and began a period of rapid growth. An indication of the scale of this growth is given by the record of the total amount invested by venture capital funds in the UK from 1985 (under £280 million) to 1993 (over £10 billion).

The growth of the market was assisted by a combination of factors which produced a very favourable environment in which the venture capital industry flourished. The first of these was the political encouragement given to small businesses and to entrepreneurial talent – the enterprise culture valued by the Conservative government. Small businesses were promoted, partly as a way to help and sustain the economic recovery of the 1980s, and partly as a way to bring down the level of unemployment. The government introduced the Business Expansion Scheme (BES), which encouraged long-term private investment in small firms through tax incentives, and the Loan Guarantee Scheme to help people who were unemployed set themselves up in business. This scheme has now been withdrawn.

Another very important factor which encouraged the growth

of the venture capital market was the favourable supply and demand situation that existed for such funding. The number of business start-ups and management buy-outs increased during the mid-eighties, thanks to the recovery of the UK economy after the recession of the early 1980s. This coincided with the prolonged bull share market, which made long-term, riskier investments increasingly attractive. The industry was further helped by the establishment of the British Venture Capital Association (BVCA) in early 1983 which served to increase awareness and co-ordination of the industry. The BVCA provides a representative voice for Britain's venture and development capitalists, and is the central reference point for those seeking venture capital. The objectives of the BVCA are given as: 'to act as a focus of members' views and interests; to provide a regular forum for the exchange of views among members; and to develop and maintain the highest standard of professional practice among members' (BVCA, 1988).

The BVCA has generated more awareness and acceptance of the industry which has contributed to its growth, with the number of members growing from 40 founder members in 1983 to a reported 125 full members and 57 associate members in March 1990.

Further helpful factors include a general change in attitudes in the UK. Historically, people in the UK have been very much averse to risk and tend to go for safer options, unlike many other countries. This meant that venture capital, which is in fact risk capital, was avoided to a great extent. However, general attitudes have been changing and it was gradually seen as more acceptable to take greater risks in order to achieve greater returns. Coupled with this was an increase in entrepreneurial attitudes, with more acceptance of setting up one's own business and 'failure' being accepted to a greater extent. The ability of a company to buy back its own shares has also increased the attractiveness of venture capital.

A final influential factor was the development of the share markets early in the eighties. The setting up of the Unlisted Securities Market (USM) in 1981, and later the Third Market in 1987, gave venture capitalists more, less-demanding markets in terms of trading records, capitalization, and so on, on which to sell their shares in the companies funded, and, of course, to realize their investments. Both these markets are now defunct owing either to stock market volatility or more stringent listing requirements. A new enterprise market is being discussed by the Stock Exchange with interested parties.

This brings up to date the major changes which have affected the venture capital industry. The boom in venture capital having appeared to slacken off slightly, has experienced a resurgence and the venture capital industry remains a major part of the economy through the continuing economic difficulties of the recession.

It is paradoxical that in spite of the growth of the venture capital industry in the last ten years or so, the problems for businesses of raising relatively small amounts of high-risk capital has not diminished to any great extent.

It is generally agreed that pre-start-up, or seed capital (which is used to turn a prototype product or plan into a going business concern), of less than £100 000 is extremely hard to raise. Funding for technological projects also continues to be difficult to come by. The problems are partly caused by the fact that evaluating and monitoring these investments can cost venture capitalists rather more than any returns they might receive.

The real growth of the venture capital market has occurred in the areas of management buy-out and buy-in funding, and expansion and secondary-purchase financing. In 1988 only 7% of the total amount invested in the market went to fund start-ups and other early-stage projects but in 1993, 19% of total investment was at an early stage (236 proposals accepted). In contrast, management buy-outs and acquisitions accounted for 62% of the total funds invested with a 38% increase in the average size of MBO financing from £2.4 million in 1992 to £3.3 million in 1993, and the remaining 31% went to expansion and secondary-purchase projects. Consumer related businesses are the largest sector for the Venture Fund 32% of investment total. Technology and life science businesses (computer, electronics, research and biotechnology) grew sharply in 1993 to £268 million.

TYPES OF INVESTMENT

The venture capital industry is often thought of as providing capital only to new ventures. While it does fulfil this role, other types of investment are also provided, most of which fall into five principal categories.

Start-up

Start-up financing (or seed capital, as it is sometimes called), which will also be taken to include early-stage financing, is where the venture capitalist provides capital to businesses at the start or early stages of their life so that the idea of the entrepreneur can be turned into business. The amounts involved are quite small, and entrepreneurs will sometimes provide these funds themselves or from family or friends because of this. This is the riskiest form of venture capital since the concept, the technology, the entrepreneur, and the market are all unproven. For these reasons, and because of the high costs involved in making the deal compared with the amount invested, this form of capital has been in short supply, which has led to both criticism of the industry and attempts to bring in more seed capital.

Development capital

This is where funds are injected into an already established business with a proven track record which wishes to develop and expand further. This type of capital is, therefore, sometimes called expansion capital. As the business has a track record and has been trading, this type of finance is much less risky as the venture capitalist has data from which an appraisal may be made. This investment area has attracted a greater amount of funds than start-up financing.

Management buy-out (MBO)

The term 'management buy-out' refers to a situation where the management team of the company concerned buy out the owners of the company and require capital to help them do this. A number of factors influence the managers' decision to adopt a buy-out policy: they may not want to remain only managers of the business; the owners may be selling it anyway; if the company is a subsidiary, the holding company may not want to operate in the industry sector any more or may simply require the cash from the sale; or the management may see the possibility of better opportunities without the constraints of the owners.

Also included in this area of financing is the management buy-in (MBI), which is where a management team from outside the company buy it out and become the management.

Due to the relatively short time to realization of the investment, which is less risky than other funding exercises, this area of venture capital funding has seen rapid growth. However, there have been criticisms that this does not really constitute venture capital, notwithstanding the fact that it is undertaken by venture capital firms.

Rescue capital

This type of financing is supplied to companies in difficulties with the hope and intention of rescuing them. Other terms used to describe this sort of funding include 'recovery' or 'turnaround' financing. The venture capitalist may undertake this sort of financing when opportunities are seen to revitalize or change the management and return the company to profitability. Some venture capitalists have even employed insolvency specialists to identify and manage such investments.

TYPES OF VENTURE CAPITAL FUNDS AVAILABLE

There are approximately 150 venture capital funds listed in the Stoy Hayward (1988) directory *Sources of Venture and Development Capital in the United Kingdom*. These may be divided into various categories: captive institutional funds, independent funds, BES funds, and government/local authority sponsored funds.

Captive funds

Captive venture capital funds are normally subsidiaries of other UK financial institutions, such as the major banks, insurance companies, pension funds, and so forth. These funds include 3i plc (owned by the Bank of England and the six largest clearing banks in the country), County Nat West Ventures Ltd, Midland Montagu Ventures Ltd, and CIN Industrial Investments.

Most captive funds are open-ended, that is, they do not have a predetermined size or duration, and they derive most of their investment funds from their parent organizations. Captive funds tend to make a proportion of their investments in the form of debt financing rather than pure equity capital. This is because the liability structures of their parent companies often require them to produce some degree of running yield or return on investment, rather than just capital growth.

Independent funds

Independent funds raise their capital for investments from a wide variety of different sources. Table 6.2 gives the detailed breakdown of these sources.

Table 6.2   Sources of capital of independent funds

	Percentage of capital committed				
	1984	1985	1986	1987	1988
UK Pension funds	40	40	41	33	37
Foreign institutions	10	21	12	36	26
UK insurers and fund managers	18	19	20	16	19
Private individuals/family trusts	19	13	15	4	11
Industrial corporations	9	4	4	4	6
UK Banks	1	1	6	6	–
Others	3	2	2	2	1
Total amount (£m)	231	278	239	684	612

Source: *UK Venture Capital Journal,* Venture Economics Ltd, London

Generally, these venture capital funds are closed-ended, and their managers often follow specific investment strategies. The funds committed by investors are drawn upon as and when profitable projects arise. The trend recently has been for the venture capital fund to be liquidated after a specified time (usually between seven and ten years) and for the proceeds to be divided among the fund's investors, rather than being reinvested in new projects. Most investments through independent funds are made via equity stakes in the enterprises and, unlike captive funds, independent venture capitalists do not usually need to make running returns on their investments.

Business Expansion Scheme funds

Capital is invested in the BES by individual small investors and it is then invested in those businesses which qualify under the BES rules. Companies with a USM or full stock market listing do not qualify for funding under this scheme, but other established firms as well as new businesses do.

The BES started life as the Business Start-up Scheme (BSS) in March 1981. The scheme provides individuals with income tax relief at their marginal rate of tax for investments of up to £40 000 per annum. This offer is attractive in terms of tax relief for higher payers, but has become less so with the top rate being reduced. The 1988 Budget also introduced a £500 000 annual investment limit for each investee company.

To qualify for this relief there are a number of rules with which the investee company must comply: it must be a UK resident company; it must be an unlisted company; it must not be a subsidiary; it must be in the qualifying trades; the company interest in land must be less than 50% of the value of its assets; and the shares must be 'eligible' and acquired by subscription. The legislation involved is complex, and the BES has not therefore proved too successful.

Government/Local Authority funds

State-owned development funds, such as the Welsh Development Agency, the Scottish Development Agency, and English Estates, invest in specific regions or industries to encourage economic growth and regeneration, and they are financed by central or local government grants.

The market shares of the different types of venture capital funds are shown in Table 6.3.

Table 6.3   Investments by types of fund

| | *Percentage of total investment* | | | | |
	1984	*1985*	*1986*	*1987*	*1988*
Captive funds	43	43	42	25	31
Independent funds	34	40	49	68	66
BES funds	20	14	8	6	2
Government/Local Authority funds	3	3	1	1	1

Source: *UK Venture Capital Journal*, Venture Economics Ltd, London

Corporate venturing

Corporate venturing is a form of venture capital funding under which a large, established company takes a minority equity stake in a small firm in order to fund and encourage product development and innovation. This practice is very much more common in the USA and in Europe than it is in the UK, where only a very few companies (such as Shell, BOC, and BP) carry it out.

European Community funds

Two venture capital funds recently set up by the European Commission also deserve a mention. Start-up and early-stage funding is as difficult to raise in Europe generally as it is in the UK. For this reason the Commission has set up a Seed Capital Project, which supports 24 new pre-start-up funds across the EC, in order to encourage private, cross-border investment in new ventures.

The other initiative is European Capital. This provides investment subsidies ranging from 4% to 50% (the latter for seed capital investments) to financial institutions to encourage them to finance more cross-border high-tech projects.

CONDUCTING THE BUSINESS

The venture capital business is typically conducted in the following way. Initially, venture capital funds receive proposals from entrepreneurs requiring the capital in the form of a business plan. This business plan gives details about the business, including the background of the entrepreneur, previous experience and training, the products and services of the business, the management and organization of the business, markets and marketing, method of operation, and financial information. The amount of information in each section will differ depending on how developed the business is; for example, past sales data will be included if the business has already undertaken some selling.

Venture capital firms receive a great many proposals, all of which are given an initial screening, which simply involves reading through them. Probably around 75% of the proposals will be rejected at this stage, with the others going on to a subsequent detailed due diligence process. This detailed analysis includes appraisal of the past performance of the business where applicable, analysis of the market potential and the competition, and analysis of the expected return.

The most important factor in the appraisal of projects, however, is commonly said to be management. Peter Owen (1987) maintains that:

> It is sometimes said that there are five key ingredients to success in starting a new business:
> 1 The Management
> 2 The Management
> 3 The Management
> 4 The Market
> 5 The Product

Thus the venture capitalists are more interested in the skills, experience, and dedication of the entrepreneur than in almost anything else, and the investment deals which tend to work best are the ones where it is seen as a sort of partnership between the parties.

It may be around only 3% of the proposals received which make it past the due diligence process and are invested in by the firm. Some funds have particular experience and knowledge in particular areas and may favour investments where they can add a great deal to the business, while others are general funds looking for any good proposals.

The terms required by the venture capital firms also vary greatly. As a general rule, no single venture capital investor will seek to take a controlling interest in investee companies. The interest may, however, range from very little to as much as 50%, depending upon what the venture capitalist requires. The venture capitalist can use one or a number of financing instruments to invest in the company's equity. The different instruments have different levels of risk attached, and include the following.

1. Deferred (ordinary) shares, where the ordinary share rights are deferred for a period of years until some future event.
2. Ordinary shares, with full equity and voting rights from the start but no dividend commitment.
3. Preferred ordinary shares, usually with full voting and equity rights, but often with a modest fixed dividend right.
4. Preference shares, which rank ahead of all types of ordinary share on liquidation. These may be wholly or partly convertible into ordinary shares, irredeemable or more frequently redeemable, and also participating in future profits. The conversion of preference shares into ordinary is often used as a mechanism to maintain the value of the total equity stake. This is known as a 'ratchet' and is usually structured so as to increase the investing institution's equity stake on a sliding scale if the company fails to achieve pre-set performance targets.
5. Convertible loan stock, which is debt, usually long term, until converted into ordinary shares.

These instruments can be used in combination, the make-up of which will depend upon the requirements of the individual venture capitalist and the type of business in which the investment is made.

EXIT ROUTES

Ultimately the venture capitalist requires the investment to be realized. Substantial returns are expected, though where there is the possibility of future growth the full holding may not be realized. The two main exit routes are involuntary and voluntary. Involuntary exits are mainly effected through receivership or liquidation and occur when the business can no longer trade without incurring substantial losses. Voluntary exits offer more choice:

(*a*) A trade sale to a third party;
(*b*) A repurchase of the shares by the entrepreneur, either directly as an individual or by the company;
(*c*) A share quotation, either through a full stock market listing, on the USM, or the over-the-counter market.

Trade sale

This has historically been the most popular exit route for venture capitalists as it is generally expected that this will produce the highest exit price, partly because corporate buyers tend to perceive benefits from merging the business with their own activities which would be lost on public shareholders. A trade sale involves the sale of the venture capitalist's shares to an acquirer outside the business. The initiative will rest with the potential acquirer to come forward to purchase the shares. Although this is the most popular exit route, because the incoming investor will usually be passive and unlikely to be expert in the field of business, sale prices tend to be influenced by the fashion appeal of that particular industry sector.

Repurchase

Following the Companies Act 1981, it became possible for a company to buy back its own shares from shareholders; prior to this it was only possible in exceptional circumstances to issue and redeem certain classes of preferred or preference shares, but even then with stringent rules attached. The Companies Act 1981 introduced the facility to issue redeemable shares of any class, giving conditions to be complied with when repurchasing the shares which were not too restrictive. This has become a real option for venture capitalists when considering an exit route.

Public share quotation

A full stock market listing involves the shares of the business being sold to the public at a quoted price through the stock market. In addition to the venture capitalist realizing the investment, the company receives a stock market listing which adds prestige which can benefit the business. However, very few companies backed by venture capitalists will be in a position to comply with the requirements for a full listing (detailed in Chapter 3), so this is not a common exit route.

Unlisted securities market (USM) quotation

The phasing-out of the USM is creating a problem for exit planning. However, the proposed enterprise market which will operate independently of the Stock Exchange, may provide a suitable alternative.

The 'over-the-counter' (OTC) market

The OTC market evolved in the 1920s in the USA and was introduced in the UK in late 1971 by Granville & Co. Ltd. It met the situation where institutions had been reluctant to invest in unlisted securities because of difficulties of selection, monitoring, and problem-solving. Granville's OTC market provided these services in order to make the investment more attractive. However, the OTC market has gained a reputation for poor investor protection standards and low-quality companies, and consequently is not a popular form of sale.

The 'living dead'

There is another alternative to the involuntary and voluntary exits already outlined. Colloquially named 'living dead' companies, which will neither make nor lose significant sums of money, lock the investor in so that invested funds may not be recycled.

THE DRAWBACKS OF USING VENTURE CAPITAL FUNDING

There are drawbacks for managers seeking risk capital from the venture capitalists. It is very difficult to obtain; estimates vary, but one venture capitalist has estimated that only 10% of business plans submitted receive more than a first reading, and only 10% of those eventually receive financial backing. Venture capital is also very costly. Fund managers often require an internal rate of return of between 40% and 50% over the life of their investment (usually about five to seven years).

With investments normally being made in the form of equity capital, venture capital financing also means that the firm's owners have to be prepared to surrender their previous total ownership and control of their business. Managers may also have to give up some strategic control over the business, depending upon how involved the venture capitalist becomes.

THE ADVANTAGES OF VENTURE CAPITAL FUNDING

The major advantage of venture capital is simply the fact that it's there, and attempts to fill a gap in the capital markets by providing the sort of financing that it does. Without using this particular form of risk capital, many new, small and innovative businesses would never have even a chance of success.

CONCLUSION

In times of recession, as rates of return become more difficult to achieve, the venture capital industry itself faces periods of slower growth and lower returns. It seems likely that as long as there is a reasonable return on investment, funds will continue to be attracted. After periods of sustained economic growth, resulting in increased competition and a larger number of venture capital organizations in the market, the almost guaranteed success of the project supported by venture capital diminishes.

The consequence of restructuring and consolidation within the industry may well result in venture capitalists being more concerned and willing to devote more time to monitoring companies and helping them through recessionary times.

Surveys reported in the *Financial Times* (1990), the *Evening Standard* (1991), and the *Independent* (1990) suggest that rescue and turnaround deals may well prove to be an area of greater opportunities for venture capital. Managers may look for experience and expertise to come with the financing package; indeed, many companies on the verge of receivership have been rescued in this way.

REFERENCES

BVCA (1988) *Report on Investment Activity 1988*, British Venture Capital Association, London.

Lorenz, T. (1985) *Venture Capital Today – a guide to the venture capital market in the UK*, Woodhead-Faulkner, Cambridge.

Pratt, G. (1990) 'Venture Capital in the United Kingdom', *Bank of England Quarterly Bulletin*, February 1990, pp. 78–83.

Shilson, D. (1984) 'Venture Capital in the UK', *Bank of England Quarterly Bulletin*, June 1984, pp. 207–11.

Stoy Hayward (1988) *Sources of Venture and Development Capital in the United Kingdom*, Stoy Hayward, London.

Evening Standard, 'Venture Capital 1991', 28 January 1991.

Financial Times venture capital survey, 26 November 1990.

Independent venture capital survey, 14 March 1990.

CHAPTER SEVEN

Foreign exchange markets

INTRODUCTION

In March 1991 it was reported that 'Allied-Lyons, one of Britain's most staid and reputable food and drink companies, has lost £150 million on speculative deals in the foreign exchange markets. The losses have forced the resignation of the group's finance director' (*Guardian*, 20 March 1991). This report highlights two important points. Firstly, there is a need for managers within any company which carries out business in more than one country to have a sound knowledge of foreign exchange markets. This is true not only for large multinational companies which have plants and offices in many countries, but also for relatively small companies which have modest international links. Secondly, it is imperative to identify the dangers which can arise from foreign exchange transactions. The report emphasizes the particular problems associated with speculative deals.

The post-war period has been characterized by a rise in the value of international business as firms increasingly recognized the profit potential offered by overseas markets. Until the early 1970s this business was carried out against a background of relatively stable foreign exchange rates, following the agreement reached at Bretton Woods in 1944. However, over the last twenty years exchange rates have become much more volatile, with the result that international business has become relatively more risky as potential profits can disappear completely by sudden movements in those rates. In response to this there has been an increase in the range and complexity of financial instruments available to managers carrying out transactions in more than one currency. The main purpose of these instruments has been to allow firms to reduce their risk by hedging, but as the *Guardian* report demonstrates these instruments can also be used for speculative purposes. The changes which have occurred since the early 1970s mean that it is important that managers and investors have an understanding of foreign exchange markets, their associated risks, and the means by which those risks can be reduced.

FOREIGN EXCHANGE RATES

Over recent years it has become common for the media to present the main exchange rates and changes in those rates from the previous day. For example, it may be announced that the pound sterling has fallen one cent against the United States dollar to $1.62. What this means is that it is possible to exchange £1 for $1.62, whereas previously $1.63 would have been received in return for £1.

A foreign exchange rate is simply the price of one currency expressed in terms of another currency. Thus, in the above example the price of £1 in dollars is $1.62. Alternatively we can say that the price of $1 is £0.617 (the result of dividing 1 by 1.62), so it costs almost 62p to buy one dollar. Similarly, it is possible to talk about other exchange rates. For example, if 2.94 Deutschmarks can be purchased for £1, then DM1 costs approximately 34p.

Taking the £/$ exchange rate and the £/DM rate enables us to determine the cross rate or $/DM rate. Since £1 has a value of $1.62 and DM2.94, it follows that $1.62 has a value of DM2.94. Thus the $/DM rate is approximately DM1.815 per dollar.

If this relationship did not hold then arbitrageurs would carry out profitable transactions bringing the exchange rates back into equilibrium. For example, take the case where the

£/$ exchange rate is 1.62, the £/DM rate is 2.94 and the $/DM rate is 1.83. If these rates hold then a 'money machine' exists. An arbitrageur can sell £1m, receiving in return $1.62m. These dollars can be used to buy DM2.9646m which can then be converted back into sterling, yielding £1 008 367. Thus a riskless profit of £8367 has been earned. By repeating the transactions more riskless profits can be generated. Clearly, such a situation cannot continue, since somebody is losing out. The existence of arbitrageurs ensures that exchange rates are aligned both in terms of cross rates and in terms of rates across the world. Hence, for example, the £/$ rate must be the same in London and New York.

Exchange rates are quoted continuously, and changes in those rates are almost constant. The factors determining exchange rates are discussed later in this chapter. A currency is said to have depreciated when more of that currency is required to purchase a unit of the other currency. For example, a change in the £/$ exchange rate from 1.64 to 1.62 means that the £ has depreciated, since it now requires more pounds (0.617) than previously (0.610) to buy $1. In contrast, the dollar has appreciated against the pound.

The exchange rates typically quoted in the media are rates of exchange where immediate delivery of the currency is required. This is known as the 'spot' rate. In practice, the spot rate is today's rate of exchange for delivery of a currency in two days' time.

In addition to the spot rate there are also forward rates of exchange. A forward rate is a rate of exchange agreed today, where delivery of the currency is required at some point in the future. Typically, forward rates are quoted for delivery of the currency in 30 days, 90 days, and 180 days, although for the major currencies longer forward rates are quoted. The difference between the spot rate and the forward rate will depend on the expected movements in currency rates in the future. If it is expected that the pound will appreciate against the foreign currency then the forward rate will reflect this. For example, if the £/$ spot rate is 1.62 and the pound is expected to appreciate in the future, then the forward rate might be 1.635. In this case the forward rate is at a discount to the spot rate (it requires £0.612 to buy $1 forward, compared with £0.617 to buy $1 spot).

The majority of forward contracts require delivery on a specified date, but it is possible to enter into a forward option contract where delivery takes place between two dates (for example, between 1st and 10th of a particular month). This type of contract is useful where a firm does not know the precise date on which foreign currency will be received.

It is worth noting that the only difference between a spot transaction and a forward transaction relates to the date of settlement. Both transactions involve the purchase of a currency at an agreed rate and on an agreed date. However, since the agreed date for spot transactions differs from that for forward transactions the spot exchange rate is likely to differ from the forward rate.

Swap transactions can also take place with foreign currency. A swap transaction occurs when there is both a purchase and a sale of a foreign currency at the same time. An example of a swap transaction is where a currency is purchased spot and sold forward simultaneously.

THE FOREIGN EXCHANGE MARKET

Unlike the stock market the foreign exchange market does not constitute a centralized marketplace. Rather, it is a world-wide market, where the participants are linked by a highly sophisticated telephone and telex system.

Essentially, there are two parts to the market: firstly, there is the inter-bank market, which is a wholesale market in which major banks and specialized brokers deal. Inter-bank market transactions are for large sums of money (typically multiples of $1m). Secondly, there is the retail market, where banks deal with their clients. In the retail market transactions can be for any amount, the value depending on the needs of the client.

The foreign exchange market is where foreign exchange transactions are carried out and exchange rates determined.

The foreign exchange market therefore allows individuals and organizations to transfer purchasing power between countries, and in this way the foreign exchange market facilitates international trade. In addition, the means for managing foreign exchange risk (forwards, futures, and options) are part of this market. The main means by which foreign exchange risk can be hedged are discussed later in the chapter.

It is estimated that $200 billion of foreign currency is traded each day on the foreign exchange market.

EXCHANGE RATES IN THE POST-WAR YEARS

In order to understand the current state of the foreign exchange markets it is useful to review briefly the post-war history of those markets. In this way the volatility of exchange rates since the early 1970s can be better understood. The post-war international monetary system was established as a result of the Bretton Woods agreement of 1944. In addition to establishing the International Monetary Fund and the World Bank, the agreement fixed all exchange rates *vis-à-vis* the US dollar. Since the dollar was linked to gold (the dollar was convertible at $35 per ounce of gold) all currencies were (indirectly) fixed in terms of gold. All the major trading nations agreed to maintain these fixed exchange rates, with only small changes being permitted. In spite of there being periodic devaluation and revaluation of currencies the agreement led to a period of stable exchange rates throughout the 1950s and into the next decade.

However, the 1960s saw increasing pressure being placed on the dollar, in particular due to concerns regarding conversion of the dollar into gold. This pressure culminated in the devaluation of the dollar against gold in 1971, with the Smithsonian agreement of December of that year setting the dollar at $38 per ounce of gold. However, in spite of this devaluation and simultaneous revaluation of other currencies, the fixed exchange rate system remained under pressure and in 1973 a system of floating exchange rates was adopted. Under a floating exchange rate regime exchange rates are determined by market forces and thus fluctuate with supply and demand. With the exception of those currencies participating in the Exchange Rate Mechanism (ERM) of the European Monetary System (EMS), floating exchange rates have remained to the present date.

The nine members of the European Economic Community established the EMS in 1979 with the creation of a new currency, the European currency unit (ECU). The ECU is not a 'hard' currency, that is to say, it is not a currency in circulation. The ERM is a part of the EMS under which the participating currencies (the UK did not join the ERM until October 1990 and left in September 1992) are fixed relative to each other. Some movement is allowed in the exchange rates across member countries, but this is limited to a small deviation from the central rate. For example while the UK was in ERM the central rate for the £/DM exchange was DM2.95. The pound could vary from approximately DM2.77 to DM3.13. As currencies approach the limit of their band the relevant countries must take action to ensure that the exchange rate stays within the allowed range. This system of (relatively) fixed exchange rates only applies to currencies participating in the ERM. Hence the currencies in the ERM, still float against the dollar, the yen, and all other currencies outside the ERM. Thus the ERM is a system of jointly floating exchange rates, and the international monetary system as a whole can be viewed as a system of floating exchange rates with certain institutional constraints.

The major impact of foreign exchange markets on firms over recent years was the increased volatility in exchange rates resulting from the move in the 1970s from fixed to floating rates. With this increased volatility came increased uncertainty regarding transactions requiring the use of a foreign currency. One of the major arguments put forward in favour of the UK joining the ERM was the greater certainty which it gives to businesses in planning their international transactions, at least within the EEC. However, there is still considerable scope for exchange rate fluctuation impacting on the profitability of overseas business.

WHAT DETERMINES EXCHANGE RATES?

It is useful for investors and managers who carry out foreign exchange transactions to have an understanding of the principles underlying exchange rate determination. Although these principles are best explained in a simplified, notional framework they have important practical implications for the behaviour of participants in foreign exchange markets. In particular, they can help managers understand the means by which risks can be hedged.

At the simplest level it can be said that exchange rates are determined by the total demand for, and supply of, different currencies. The market forces evident in foreign exchange markets lead to adjustments in exchange rates until demand and supply are equilibrated. In turn the demand for, and supply of, different currencies depends upon the requirements of firms and individuals, whether they be for business purposes, currency speculation, or overseas travel, and upon the behaviour of governments in the foreign exchange markets. Since these requirements are continuously changing, demand and supply is also continuously changing and hence exchange rates in a freely floating system will move with these changes. However, it is necessary to look beyond this statement that exchange rates are determined by demand and supply, in order to understand the factors affecting that demand and supply and hence exchange rates. This is best understood by considering the main international parity relationships.

PURCHASING POWER PARITY

Purchasing power parity (PPP), also known as the law of one price, is concerned with the relationship between exchange rates and inflation. It has as its starting point the idea that internationally traded commodities should cost the same in every country. Thus exchange rates should be such that goods which cost £100 in the UK should cost the equivalent of £100 in any other currency. If this is not the case people will seek to buy the goods in the country where they are cheapest. Consider a situation in which the £/$ exchange rate is 2.20, and where some particular good costs £100 in the UK and $200 in the US. Clearly, the law of one price does not hold. The result of this will be that people in the UK will sell pounds, buy dollars, and purchase the good for £90.91 (i.e. $200/$2.20). This process increases demand for dollars and the supply of pounds, which will increase the cost of dollars. The process will continue until the £/$ rate is 2.

This strict absolute version of PPP clearly does not hold in practice, due to factors such as taxes, import duties, and transportation costs. Nevertheless, PPP has implications for the impact of inflation on exchange rates. The relative version of PPP does not require prices to be the same in all countries, but rather argues that differential inflation rates between countries will lead to an offsetting change in exchange rates. Consider an example where the £/$ exchange rate is in equilibrium at $2 to the £. If the inflation rate in the UK is expected to be 10% while that in the US is expected to be 5%, then PPP holds that expected exchange rates will reflect this. Before inflation, goods that cost £100 in the UK will require $200 to purchase. After inflation the goods in the UK will cost £110 and relative PPP holds that the exchange rate will adjust so that this requires $210. Hence the £/$ exchange rate is 210/110 = 1.91. If this did not happen, and given that the exchange rates were in equilibrium prior to the inflation, UK exports would be less competitive in the US and imports from the US would be relatively cheaper. Thus fewer pounds would be demanded by US importers and more dollars would be demanded by UK importers. These changes in demand will ensure PPP (at least in its relative form) will hold. Hence, changes in nominal exchange rates reflect different levels of inflation in different countries.

THE INTERNATIONAL FISHER EFFECT

The international Fisher effect builds on the view put forward in 1930 by Irving Fisher that nominal interest rates comprise two parts: a real rate of return and the expected rate of inflation. Investors will expect to earn a real rate of return on their investments, and thus the higher the rate of inflation the higher must be the nominal rate of interest. Given that real rates of interest are relatively stable over time, nominal interest rates depend primarily on inflationary expectations. In addition, in a world of free-flowing capital, real rates of return should be equal across countries, although nominal rates of return will vary with differences in expected inflation.

The international Fisher effect states that differences in interest rates across countries will be offset by an equal and opposite change in the spot exchange rate. This condition must hold to ensure that real rates of return in different countries are equal.

Consider an investor with £1000 to invest. The UK interest rate is 12% while that in the US is 7%. The current exchange rate is 1.75. The investor can either invest the £1000 in the UK, yielding £1120 in a year's time, or convert the £1000 into $1750 and invest this in the US, yielding $1872.50 next year. If the spot rate in a year's time is still 1.75 then the investor will only receive £1070 from converting $1872.50. The international Fisher effect holds that the spot exchange rate will change to $1.672. The depreciation in the pound is offset by a higher nominal rate of return in the UK.

INTEREST RATE PARITY

Interest rate parity (IRP) says that the differential in interest rates between two countries must be equal to the differential between the forward and spot exchange rates for the currencies of the two countries. If IRP does not hold then riskless profit opportunities would exist. For example, take the case where interest rates are 12% in the UK and 7% in the US. The current

£/$ exchange rate is 2 and the one year forward rate is 1.95. An investor in the US could borrow $2000, which requires repayment of $2140 in one year's time. The investor could convert the $2000 into £1000 and invest at 12% yielding £1120 in one year. If the investor also buys dollars forward at 1.95 then £1120 × 1.95 = $2184 will be received. The loan plus interest can be repaid and a riskless profit of $44 received.

In practice, there are many investors with millions of pounds worth of funds to invest in short-term, interest-bearing assets. These investors are continually on the lookout for profitable opportunities and therefore monitor national interest rates very closely. If IRP did not hold investors would swiftly move funds to benefit from the riskless profit opportunities. These movements would impact on spot and forward rates, ensuring that IRP is enforced. In other words, market forces will ensure that profit opportunities are eroded.

THE RELATIONSHIP BETWEEN THE FORWARD RATE AND THE EXPECTED SPOT RATE

The last of the parity relationships states that the forward exchange rate is equal to the expected value of the spot exchange rate for the time of forward delivery. Hence, if the £/$ one year forward rate is 1.9 this means that market participants expect the £/$ spot exchange rate in one year's time to be 1.9. Any new information which impacts on expectations regarding the future spot rate will also impact on the forward rate. The main implication of this relationship is that on average it will not be profitable to try to beat the market by forecasting exchange rates, and hence the market does not reward investors for carrying foreign exchange risk.

THE RELATIONSHIPS IN PRACTICE

Clearly, in practice there are imperfections which prevent these relationships holding precisely. In particular, some of the relationships depend upon expectations of future inflation and future spot rates which are uncertain in practice. In addition, transportation costs, import duties, and taxes exist. Nevertheless, there is considerable evidence to suggest that in the long run these relationships do hold true.

FOREIGN EXCHANGE RISK

When firms become involved in business which requires transactions in more than one currency, there is inevitably an extra dimension to the risks which they face. In particular, business opportunities which appear profitable at one set of exchange rates may be very unprofitable in the wake of adverse movements in those rates.

In much of the post-war period businesses could plan ahead, fairly confident that exchange rates were fixed. However, under the fixed rate regime, when devaluation or revaluation occurred, the size of the movement was relatively large. With the move to floating exchange rates these 'step' changes have been avoided, but managers can be much less confident about future exchange rates. Entry into the ERM gave some bounds to the movement of sterling *vis-à-vis* EC member currencies. Nevertheless, there is still enough scope for changes in rates to make apparently profitable business opportunities unprofitable. In addition, the UK still had floating rates relative to non-EC currencies such as the dollar. Indeed, in the first six months of 1991 the £/$ exchange rate ranged from 2.00 to 1.6125. Clearly, then, the risk associated with exchange rate movements is considerable, and it is therefore necessary for managers to be aware both of the risks associated with foreign currency transactions and of the methods available for reducing or dealing with those risks.

Exchange rate risk occurs whenever a firm or individual agrees to the settlement of a financial obligation at a fixed amount of a foreign currency. Such agreements can arise when a firm sells goods to or buys goods from abroad for settlement at a later date, or when funds are borrowed or lent in a foreign currency.

Obviously, the easiest way to avoid such risk exposure is to try to avoid having to settle financial obligations in a foreign currency, so that all lending and borrowing could be done in domestic currency. Similarly, when negotiating a contract with an overseas business, whether it is to buy or to sell, a manager could insist that settlement is made in the company's home currency. However, a major problem arises when adopting such an approach. By insisting on settlement in domestic currency the manager may lose business, or be required to pay a higher price for supplies. The counterparty to any business transaction is likely to be equally keen to avoid exchange rate risk, and if a competitor is willing to quote in the purchasing firm's currency the firm quoting in its domestic currency will be at a disadvantage.

An alternative is to insist on cash when the order is placed since the spot exchange rate is known at that time. However, this again runs the risk of losing business or being charged a higher price or having to reduce the price to compensate for the counterparty accepting the risk. Hence, it is often necessary for firms to agree to settlement in a foreign currency at a future date.

For some firms which operate in many countries and hence carry out transactions in numerous currencies it is possible to adopt a policy of assuming that gains from advantageous currency movements will, over the longer term, balance out against losses from adverse currency movements. However, such a policy is not appropriate for many firms, and it is therefore necessary to find alternative means by which foreign exchange risk can be eliminated or reduced.

HEDGING FOREIGN EXCHANGE RISK

A firm which wishes to avoid an unhedged position with regard to foreign exchange exposure has a number of alternative means by which to achieve its objective. In principle, hedging can be achieved in the forward market, the money markets, or by using futures or options contracts. In addition, a system of leads and lags can be adopted to manage foreign exchange exposure. In practice, options markets are best suited to particular situations (these are dealt with in Chapter 9) and futures contracts are used much less than forward markets in the UK. Indeed, due to the strength of the over-the-counter forward markets in the UK, the London International Financial Futures Exchange (LIFFE) has withdrawn its currency futures contracts, though currency futures can still be purchased through US markets. Emphasis will therefore be placed on the use of forward and money markets.

Forward contracts are the most obvious means by which to hedge against foreign exchange risk. A firm which is due to settle a financial obligation at a future date in a foreign currency, whether it be a receivable or a payable, can enter into a simple hedging contract, buying or selling forward on the foreign exchange market. An example helps to illustrate the use of forward contracts. Consider a UK firm which signs a contract to export goods to the US, with the US importer agreeing to pay $1m for the goods in one year's time. The spot exchange rate at the time of signing is $1.60 to £1. Hence, at the spot exchange rate at the time of signing, the contract will yield £625 000 for the UK exporter.

Clearly, if the exchange rate is different at the time the payment is made, then the UK firm will receive either more pounds or less pounds then the £625 000. For example, if the pound appreciates to $1.80 then only £555 556 will be received. If it depreciates to $1.40 then £714 286 will be received. Some firms may be willing to take the risk of 'losing' from adverse exchange rate movements in return for the chance of 'winning' from favourable movements. However, the firm wishes to hedge the receivable using forward markets.

The exporter therefore enters into a forward foreign currency transaction, agreeing to sell $1m against sterling in one year's time. The one-year forward rate at the time the contract is signed is $1.62 to £1. Thus the firm has locked in an amount receivable of £617 284, and whatever the spot rate at the time the $1m is due, the firm will sell dollars at $1.62 to £1. The firm has hedged against appreciation of the pound beyond $1.62 and at the same time forgone the possibility of gains if the pound depreciated over the coming year. The advantage of such a transaction is clear. The firm knows precisely the sum to be received in one year's time, and thus the risk associated with adverse foreign exchange rate movements has been removed.

One of the parity relationships presented earlier stated that the forward exchange rate is equal to the expected value of the spot exchange rate for the time of forward delivery. Belief in this parity relationship does not imply that forward contracts are unnecessary. The relationship would hold that in the example above the expected spot rate for the time at which $1m is to be received is $1.62 to £1. However, this expectation is based on the information available at the time the contract is signed. In the following year new information will continually become available which will lead to expectations changing, and it is therefore most unlikely that the spot rate will actually be $1.62 to £1 in one year's time.

Forward contracts for periods greater than a year were not available until a few years ago. This meant that firms wanting to hedge over, say, two years, could only do so by arranging a swap with another firm or financial institution with an opposite position which it wished to hedge. Arranging such deals was not always easy, but more recently forward contracts for up to five years have been available with the large banks for the main traded currencies.

An alternative to hedging in forward markets is to use money markets to achieve the same objective. This hedge will be illustrated using the same example as for the forward market hedge. In this case the hedge is achieved by the UK exporter borrowing dollars for one year. The amount to be borrowed should be such that the sum due as repayment in one year's time (principal plus interest) is equal to the amount to be received at that time. Thus, if interest rates in the US are 7% per annum the UK firm should borrow $934 579, which with 7% interest will require $1m to be repaid in a year. The sum of $934 579 should then be converted to pounds at the current exchange rate of $1.60 to £1, yielding £584 111 immediately. The $1m receivable in a year's time can be used to repay the loan. While the sum received of £584 111 is clearly less than $1m at the exchange rate of $1.60 to £1, the money has been received one year earlier and can be profitably employed in the intervening period. If interest rates in the UK are also 7% then by investing the £584 111 at this rate the firm would receive £625 000 in one year's time. However, given the forward rate of $1.62 it is more likely that UK interest rates would be below US rates. An interest rate of 5.68% would yield £617 288 in one year's time, virtually the same as the amount received from the forward contract. As long as foreign exchange markets are efficient then IRP will lead to the costs of the forward market hedge and the money market hedge being approximately equal. However, IRP relates to differences in interest rates for risk-free, interest-bearing assets, namely, government bills. The interest rates available to firms will be different from these risk-free rates, and hence the differences in the rates faced by the firm may not accord with IRP. As a consequence there may be differential costs for money market and forward market hedges. While the difference is likely to be small, it may still be large enough to make it worthwhile for managers to calculate which hedge will be cheaper.

Leading and lagging is another means by which foreign exchange risk can be managed. Leading involves a company paying its debts before they fall due in the belief that its domestic currency will depreciate before payment is due. By leading with its payment a firm will spend less of its currency to meet an obligation than will be required after depreciation. Lagging involves paying debts after they are due in the belief that the domestic currency will appreciate. In this case the foreign currency is cheaper the later the debt is paid.

Clearly, then, there are techniques available for managing foreign exchange risk. Forward markets and money markets are the most common means by which companies hedge these risks. In addition, futures and options contracts can also have a role to play, as is shown in the following chapters.

SPECULATION IN FOREIGN EXCHANGE MARKETS

This chapter opened with a report of losses made by speculation on foreign exchange markets. Speculation involves taking on additional risk in the hope of making higher profits, that is to say, trading on the basis of expectations about prices in the future. Thus, a speculator could take an unhedged position in a particular currency in the belief that the currency will move in a particular direction (either appreciate or depreciate). The speculator would then close out that position either when the rate has moved as expected (thus making a profit) or when the investor's expectations about future movements change (which may well involve losses). It should, perhaps, be self-evident that firms should not be involved with speculation, but rather should be aiming to manage the foreign exchange risks which they face.

CONCLUSION

This chapter has explained the basis of foreign exchange markets and the principles which underlie exchange rate movements. Any manager who is involved in transactions in more than one currency requires an understanding of these markets. In addition, it is essential that managers be aware of the risks associated with foreign currency transactions and the means available for reducing or eliminating those risks. The important point for all managers to appreciate is that foreign exchange risk does not have to be accepted as an inevitable part of international business.

FURTHER READING

Eiteman, D.K., and Stonehill, A.I. (1989) *Multinational Business Finance*, 5th edn, Addison-Wesley, Wokingham.

Heywood, J. (1984) *Using the Futures, Forwards and Options Markets*, A. & C. Black, London.

Solnik, B. (1989) *International Investments*, Addison-Wesley, Wokingham.

CHAPTER EIGHT

Futures markets

INTRODUCTION

The 1970s proved to be a decade of great importance to international financial markets. The changes in the financial environment in which firms operated, in particular the increased volatility of interest rates and exchange rates, resulted in a demand for financial instruments which could provide protection against such volatility. In addition to the role of forward contracts (discussed in Chapter 7) the two types of instruments which have emerged to be particularly important in this regard are options (discussed in Chapter 9) and futures, the subject of this chapter.

There is evidence that a form of futures trading took place in Amsterdam and Japan as early as the seventeenth century, but it was in the nineteenth century that futures trading began to develop into a form comparable with that undertaken now. Originally, futures trading was almost exclusively devoted to agricultural commodities due to the seasonal nature of the supply of these products, but in recent years trading in financial futures has come to be of much greater importance, with this type of futures contract accounting for over 60% of the annual volume of futures contracts traded by the end of the 1980s.

As is the case with options, Chicago was the first centre where organized financial futures trading took place. The early 1970s saw the birth of futures trading of foreign currencies following the move to floating exchange rates. In 1975 interest-bearing assets became the subject of futures trading, and the early 1980s witnessed the first trading of futures on stock indices. In addition to there being several organized futures markets in the United States, there are numerous other countries which offer these markets. Indeed, some exchanges have been established specifically for the purposes of trading in financial futures, rather than in the more traditional agricultural commodities and metals: the London International Financial Futures Exchange (LIFFE), for example, was established in 1982 and the Tokyo Financial Futures Exchange in 1985.

METHODS OF TRADING COMMODITIES AND INSTRUMENTS

Trading in futures provides a parallel market to the market for the actual physical commodity or financial instrument. Futures markets evolved for the primary purpose of improving the operations of these parallel markets. In order to have a clear understanding of the nature of futures it is necessary to distinguish between the different ways in which goods may be exchanged.

Actuals markets

As the name suggests, an actuals market is a market in which the actual physical commodity or financial instrument is traded. There are two types of actuals market, the spot market and the forward market. The spot market involves both the transfer of ownership and the delivery of the commodity or instrument on the spot, or immediately. With a forward market the transfer of ownership occurs on the spot, but delivery of the commodity or instrument does not occur until some future date.

In the case of either the spot or the forward markets the term 'market' may be somewhat misleading, in that the trading can take place anywhere. The market need not be organized or located in a particular centralized market-place. In addition, when a contract is established in the actuals market it can be specifically designed to satisfy the requirements of the parties to the contract. In the case of commodities, for example, the grade and quantity of the commodity traded can be specified, as can the place and time of delivery of the commodity. Similarly, the parties to the contract are free to settle the contract in any way which they find agreeable.

Futures markets

In contrast to the freedom to specifically design each contract traded in the actuals market, futures markets involve highly standardized contracts. These contracts allow for the frequent transfer of title and liability at any time until a future delivery date. While there are similarities between forward contracts and futures contracts, there are considerable differences, particularly in relation to the standardization of futures contracts and the fact that futures trading takes place through organized and centralized exchanges.

THE NATURE OF FUTURES

What are futures?

A futures contract is an agreement to buy or sell a standard quantity of a particular commodity or financial instrument at a future date for a price which is agreed at the time the contract is drawn up. Unlike options, a futures contract involves an obligation on the part of both the buyer and the seller to fulfil the conditions of the contract. The rest of this chapter will concentrate on financial futures, although reference will be made to commodity futures.

The use of standard contracts

The standardization of futures contracts is, perhaps, the most important factor which distinguishes futures contracts from forward contracts. Each futures contract is for a standard specified quantity. For example, each LIFFE three-month Eurodollar interest rate futures contract has a unit of trading of US $1 000 000. The contract not only specifies the quantity of the instrument in the contract, but also the quality in terms of, for example, its coupon rate and maturity. For commodities, the grade of the commodity to be delivered is specified in the contract.

The great advantage of standardized contracts is that potential buyers and sellers of the contracts can easily find out the details of the contract, whereas with forward contracts the market participants will have to acquire information about each individual contract. In addition, because futures contracts are not designed for specific parties, market participants can easily close out their position by taking an offsetting position in the market. Thus standardization increases the marketability of the contracts and hence increases liquidity within the markets.

Trading through organized exchanges

Unlike forward contracts which can be traded through any means which is agreeable to the parties involved, futures contracts are always traded through centralized, organized exchanges such as the Chicago Board of Trade or LIFFE. An exchange comprises an association of the members of the exchange and, together with professional managers, the members of the exchange are responsible for its running. The exchange does not trade in contracts itself, but rather provides the location where trading can take place within a highly organized and regulated framework.

The trading of futures and the liquidity of the market are considerably aided by the centralization of the market-place at an exchange. The market's liquidity is further enhanced by all transactions in the market and all prices being instantly available to all market participants (either through a system of open outcry or through electronic trading), and as a result large volumes of impersonal transactions can be undertaken.

The role of the clearing houses

Another of the distinctive characteristics of futures markets is the fact that a clearing house is interposed between each buyer and seller. This means that the obligation of the buyer and the seller is not to each other but rather to the clearing house. Essentially, once a buyer and a seller have been found for a contract, the clearing house takes over the role of the other parties to the transaction. Thus the clearing house is the seller of the contract to the buyer and the buyer of the contract from the seller. The financial resources of the clearing house ensure that every transaction which is carried out on the exchange is guaranteed, thus virtually eliminating the risk of default on any transaction. It is only the large volume of futures transactions which are carried out which makes the clearing house settlement procedures economically feasible. Hence, in part, it is the liquidity of the markets which enables these procedures to exist. However, by removing default risk and allowing transactions to be closed out by opposite transactions the clearing house adds to the liquidity of the markets.

Margin requirements

Since the clearing house is the guarantor of every transaction carried out on the exchange, it is obviously taking on the default risk of the opposing parties to the transactions. To protect itself from this risk and to enable it to undertake the role of guarantor to every transaction, the clearing house requires market participants to put up margin (deposit a sum of money). Whenever a contract is traded both buyer and seller are required to put up margin to give protection against adverse price movements. This margin is not a downpayment towards buying the contract, but rather is a guarantee of the market participant fulfilling the contract. This 'initial margin' is set by the clearing house, with the level depending on the volatility of the underlying instrument. The margin is quite small, normally being about 5% of the face value of the contract, but in some cases being considerably smaller.

The prices of futures contracts clearly change over time, and as a result the parties to the contracts will make (as yet unrealized) gains and losses. To protect the clearing house from such movements all open futures positions are 'marked-to-the-market' at the close of each trading day. This involves the use of 'variation margin', whereby each day's gains are added to the margin account and each day's losses subtracted from that account. The initial margin must be maintained and as a result additional funds will be required when losses are made. Since all losses are collected each day as the position is marked-to-the-market, the financial security of the clearing houses and of the exchanges is maintained. In the case where a contract is held until delivery the buyer must pay the seller the full value of the contract.

Together with the use of standard contracts, organized exchanges and clearing houses, the low margin requirements help reduce the costs of trading futures contracts. In particular, the sound organizational structure of the market keeps transaction costs relatively low, ensures asset quality, and minimizes default risk, thus making futures markets highly liquid and enabling a high volume of transactions to take place.

THE PRICING OF FUTURES CONTRACTS

In order to have a thorough knowledge of the basics of futures contracts, of their uses, and their economic functions, it is essential that the pricing of futures contracts is well understood. There will be very great differences in the factors which affect the price of cocoa futures and those affecting the price of Eurodollar futures. Indeed, even within the narrower field of financial futures, the determinants of futures prices will differ across contracts on different types of underlying instruments. Further, the way in which prices are quoted varies with the nature of the underlying instrument. In spite of these differences, however, there are factors which are common to the understanding of the pricing of all futures contracts. Given the necessarily short space which can be devoted to pricing here, consideration will be given to these common factors rather than examining the determinants of prices for different commodities and financial instruments.

The relationship between the actuals price and the futures price

It has been established that the financial instrument on which contracts are traded in the futures market is also traded in the actuals market. Hence, it is evident that the factors affecting the price of the instrument in one type of market will also affect prices in the other market. Clearly, then, there will be a relationship between prices in futures markets and prices in the actuals markets for the underlying instrument. For simplicity, we shall concentrate on the relationship between spot prices and futures prices, although it should be remembered that similar relationships may hold between forward prices and futures prices.

The basis

The 'basis' is the difference between the price of a futures contract and the price of the instrument in the spot market:

Basis = Current cash price − futures price.

When there is more than one futures contract for the same underlying instrument, with the contracts differing by their dates of expiration, then there will be a basis for each of the contracts. The basis is largely determined by expectations of what the spot price will be at the time of expiration of the futures contract. As a result, the price of futures contracts with a date of expiration a long time in the future is likely to be greater than for a contract which will expire in the near future. When this occurs the market is exhibiting a pattern of normal prices. However, this will not always be the case. For example, where the supplies of a particular commodity are expected to be higher in the future, the expected spot price will be lower further into the future and hence distant futures contracts will be priced lower than nearby contracts. In such a situation the market is said to be inverted.

More uncertainty exists the further into the future is the date of expiration, and hence there are more likely to be differences of opinion as to the future spot price at later dates. As a result, the basis is likely to be more volatile for contracts with maturity far in the future.

While the basis can either be positive or negative for different commodities and instruments, and at different times, it is the case that at the time of delivery of the contract (that is, at expiration) the futures price and the spot price must always be extremely close. Indeed, in the absence of transportation and transactions costs, the prices will be equal. If this were not the case then arbitrageurs would be able to make riskless profits, and their actions would drive the prices to equality. Hence, while the basis will vary over time, the price of the futures contract will converge on the spot price as delivery approaches and the basis thus converges to zero at expiry.

Time spreads

In addition to there being a relationship between the spot price and the futures price, there is also a relationship between the prices of futures contracts which are on the same commodity or instrument but which have different expiry dates. The difference between the prices of two such contracts is known as the time spread. (There are also spreads between the prices of futures contracts on different instruments which have the same date of expiration). The 'spread' is at the heart of speculation or trading on futures markets. Essentially, traders try to identify spreads which they believe are not justified by the relevant economic considerations. Trading will be discussed later in this chapter.

Understanding futures prices

Even within the field of financial futures, there is considerable variety in the types of contracts traded. On LIFFE, for example, futures contracts are traded on many instruments including long- and short-dated gilt-edged stocks, short-term sterling interest rates, three-month Eurodollars, three-month ECUs, US Treasury bonds, Japanese and German government bonds, and the FTSE 100 index. Although each futures contract is, by definition, standardized, a different structure exists for each of the contracts. In this section the aim is to explain the prices of futures contracts as shown in the financial press. To this end, the prices for a long gilt contract as shown in the *Financial Times* on 8 July 1994 are reproduced in Table 8.1. Gaining an understanding of these figures should give insights into the prices of different financial futures.

Table 8.1

LIFFE 9% Notional Gilt

£50 000 32nds of 100%

	Close	high	Low	Open
September	100–14	101–03	98–18	99–25
December	99–14	99–00	99–00	99–00

Estimated volume 63367
Previous day's open interest 110594

Source: Financial Times, 8 July 1994

The first point of interest concerning Table 8.1 is that the financial instrument for which futures prices are quoted is not an actual long gilt, but rather a *notional* long gilt. Hence, a gilt with exactly the same characteristics does not exist in the actuals market – there is no underlying security which is *directly* comparable to the notional gilt and hence the basis cannot be calculated directly. In this case the notional gilt is one with 10 to 15 years to maturity and offering a coupon rate of 9%. The size of the contract is shown on the second line of the table as being a nominal (face value) of £50 000. Next to the size of the contract is the 'tick', the minimum step by which the price can move. For long gilts the tick is one 32nd of 1%. Given that the contract size is £50 000, a tick represents £15.625 (£50 000 ×

1% × 1/32). In theory, the contract buyer is purchasing a nominal £50 000 of gilt-edged stock for delivery in the future. Moving now to the body of the table, four prices are shown for each contract (in other words, for contracts with different delivery dates), namely the closing price the high and low prices for the day, and the day's opening price. The prices shown are for each £100 of nominal value. For example, for the contract with maturity in September the closing price is shown as 100–14. This means that £100 nominal of the gilt costs £100 14/32. Given that the contract size is £50 000, the cost of the contract is £50 218.75 (£100 14/32 × 50 000/100). It should be remembered that on purchasing the contract only the initial margin must be paid: the initial margin for long gilts is £1000.

If interest rates rise then it is likely that the value of the contract will fall. This will occur because, with rising interest rates, fixed-interest gilt-edged stocks will fall in value. On the other hand, with falling interest rates, the value of the contract will rise. For example, if an investor purchased the September contract at 100–14 and the price of the contract rose to 104–04, the contract could be sold at 104–04 thus cancelling the contract purchased at 100–14. The profit from this is equal to 118 ticks, which has a cash value of £1843.75 (118 × £15.625). Given the low margin requirements it is possible to make a large profit while only committing a relatively small sum of money. In this case a profit of £1843.75 has been made on an investment (in terms of the initial margin) of only £1000.

In the vast majority of cases purchasers of contracts close their positions by selling an identical contract and taking the associated profit or loss. It is rare for financial futures contracts to be delivered. However, when delivery is required (that is to say, the position is not closed by an offsetting transaction) LIFFE will accept any of a variety of gilts which have between 10 and 15 years to maturity. Since the contract traded is only notional, in the case of delivery LIFFE will make adjustments to bring the various deliverable stocks which have different coupons and maturities on to a common basis for delivery.

The final two lines of Table 8.1 show the estimated volume traded that day and the open interest for the day prior to the

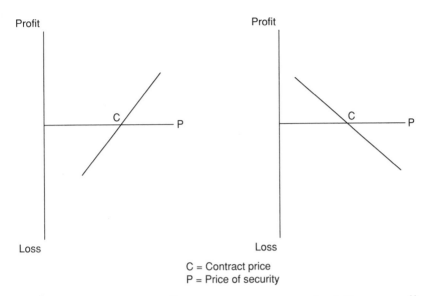

C = Contract price
P = Price of security

Figure 8.1 Buyers pay-off.   **Figure 8.2** Sellers pay-off.

day to which the other figures related. Open interest is the number of futures contracts which have not been liquidated and indicates the level of interest in the particular contract.

It is evident from this example that the figures quoted in the *Financial Times* do not tell the whole story. In particular, the margin requirements and the nominal value for which prices are quoted (in this case £100) are not shown. Full information on the different contracts can be obtained from LIFFE.

BASIC PAY-OFF POSITIONS

The pay-off associated with taking a position in the futures market can be either positive or negative. The pay-offs for buyers and sellers of futures contracts are shown in Figures 8.1 and 8.2.

The buyer of the contract has an obligation to purchase the underlying instrument at a price of C (or undertake an offsetting transaction). When the spot price is above the contract price the buyer will buy the instrument for the price C and can sell the instrument for the higher spot price, thus making a profit. When the contract price is above the spot price a loss is made by the buyer of the contract. In contrast the seller of the contract makes a profit when the contract price is above the spot price (the seller will purchase the instrument at the spot price and sell at the contract price) and a loss when the spot price is above the contract price.

Purchase of a futures contract to buy the underlying security involves taking a 'long position' in the futures market. A commitment to sell the underlying instrument involves taking a 'short position' in futures.

USERS OF FUTURES MARKETS

Financial futures markets were established with the prime objective of enabling companies and individuals to insure against the possible adverse effects of changes in interest and exchange rates. Thus, the main role of financial futures markets is the reduction of risk or 'hedging'. However, when an individual or company reduces risk by hedging, the risk is not eliminated but rather is transferred to the counterparty to the trade. This counterparty may be another hedger with opposite requirements or, more likely, it will be a speculator or 'trader'. Traders are active in the markets, not to reduce risk, but rather to take on risk in the expectation that they can profit from their activity. More specifically, traders make an assessment of current and future interest and exchange rates and attempt to trade profitably on future price changes.

Trading in futures markets

Traders or speculators become involved in any market with the primary aim of profiting from price movements in that market. Essentially, they aim to buy an asset when the price is (as they see it) low and sell that asset when they believe the price is high. Futures markets are no exception to this. Traders enter futures markets with the aim of making a profit. In their attempt to do this they are willing to take on the risk that hedgers are seeking to avoid.

Futures markets are attractive to traders for two main reasons. Firstly, the margin requirements enable traders to deal in contracts worth many times the amount of money which they need to commit – in other words, futures are highly geared. Secondly, futures markets prices are relatively volatile and movements in the basis sufficiently large for potentially high rewards to result.

Three main types of traders can be identified: scalpers, day traders, and position (or long-term) traders. The difference between these three types result from the time horizon of the traders. Scalpers have a very short time horizon, seeking to trade profitably on the basis of price movements in the next few minutes. Scalpers do not expect to make large profits on a single trade, but rather aim to profit by a few ticks per trade on a very large number of transactions. Given the large volume of transactions undertaken, and the relatively small profits per trade, it is only possible for scalpers to earn profits if they can avoid transaction costs. Scalpers are therefore typically either exchange members, or have a seat on the exchange. The actions of scalpers, although speculative, are important to futures markets since they enhance the liquidity of the market.

Day traders take a longer-term view than do scalpers, aiming to profit on transactions carried out within a trading day. Day traders are clearly looking for a lower volume of transactions than are scalpers, but aim to earn higher profits per trade. They close out their position within a trading day to avoid the possibility of substantial losses due to major price movements when the market they trade in is closed. Given that scalpers and day traders do not hold positions overnight, it should be clear that a large volume of transactions takes place in the later part of the trading day.

Position traders, or long-term traders, are those traders who are willing to have an open position overnight. Indeed, some position traders will take up a particular position, either long or short, and hold that position for several weeks. The reason for such trading is that the participants believe that over a period of time prices will move in a manner favourable to their position.

One of the riskiest types of trading strategy involves a long-term trader taking up an outright position. This involves the trader either buying or selling a particular contract and holding on to that position for a long period. Such trading can result in very high profits if prices move in the way the trader expects. However, adverse price movements can result in very large losses, since the outright position has no cover.

A less risky strategy involves taking up a spread position. Spread trading involves buying and selling two different but related futures contracts at the same time. The aim of spread trading is to make a profit on the basis of the difference between two contract prices. For example, a spread trader may take the view that the differential between the LIFFE Eurodollar and the LIFFE three-month sterling futures is greater or less than it should be. The trader will take a position whereby one of the contracts is sold and the other is purchased, profiting if the differential moves as expected. A less risky type of spread involves buying and selling the same contract, but with different delivery months. Such a spread is known as a straddle. Because it is a less risky form of spread, straddles have the advantage of reduced margins.

Clearly, from a manager's point of view, trading is not really desirable. If you want to go into futures trading, taking on increased risk, it would be desirable from the firm's standpoint if you do it with your own money. Indeed, the activities of scalpers and day traders are beyond the wherewithal of most managers. It is hedging which is of particular interest to managers.

Hedging in futures markets

Unlike traders, hedgers are concerned with the avoidance or reduction of risk even if this necessitates a potential loss of profits. Clearly, then, hedgers enter into futures transactions when they already hold a position (normally in the underlying security) which involves them in risk. Hedging can be used for reducing the risk associated with foreign exchange, interest rate and share price movements, although in practice forward markets tend to provide a better means of dealing with foreign exchange risk. The hedging of risk is achieved by the hedger (either an individual investor or a firm) taking a position that is equal and opposite to an existing position in the spot market or to a position which it is anticipated will be adopted. Essentially, then, hedging is used to reduce a risk which an investor or business is facing or will face.

While the aim of hedging is ultimately to eliminate risk, in practice this is not possible with futures: it is only possible to reduce risk. The reason for this is that futures prices may not move exactly in line with spot market movements, and hence hedgers will be exposed to any changes in the basis. However, while futures hedging cannot eliminate risk it does reduce it by converting the risk of interest rate or share price movements into the lesser risk of changes in the basis.

To help to understand the way in which futures can be used to hedge risk, consider the following example.

Example   A firm has a £3m three-month loan at a rate of 12% which is due to be rolled over on 31 August. At the beginning of May the firm is looking ahead to the planned rollover and is concerned that by the time of the rollover interest rates will have risen. In order to hedge the risk associated with a rise in interest rates, the financial manager of the firm decides to use the futures market. LIFFE's three-month sterling interest rate contract is most appropriate for the hedge.

The firm sells 6 contracts (unit of trading £500 000) at a price of 88.00. (The price of the contract is calculated as 100 minus the rate of interest. Thus with a 12% rate of interest the price is $100 - 12 = 88$. The reason for this form of pricing is so that the contract behaves in a manner similar to bonds: when interest rates rise, prices fall.) Given the date of rollover the September contract is most appropriate. A one-tick movement has a value of £12.50 (minimum price movement × unit of trading × length of contract = $0.01\% \times £500\ 000 \times 3/12$).

If the interest rate rises between now and the delivery day the price of the futures contract should fall. Let us assume that interest rates rise to 14.5% and that the futures price falls to 85.5. The firm will be in the position where it now has to pay an extra 2.5% on its loan at a cost of £18 750 (£3m × 2.5% × 3/12), but it will make a profit on closing out its futures position. It has sold 6 contracts at 88.00 and can buy them back at 85.5, a gain of 250 ticks per contract. The total gain on the futures transactions will be £18 750 (250 × £12.50 × 6). Hence the 'loss' on the rollover is matched by the gain on the futures transaction.

If the futures price moved in a way which did not exactly match the movement in spot interest rates then the hedge would be less than perfect, but none the less would reduce risk (for example, a futures price of 85.7 would yield a gain of £17 250 which covers 92% of the 'loss' on the movement in interest rates).

This example clearly illustrates the advantages of hedging. It is of course true that, had interest rates fallen rather than risen, the business would have made a loss on the futures contract, offsetting the 'gain' on the lower cost of the rollover – in other words, the cost of reducing the risk of losing is the reduction in the possibility of gaining. For most firms this is a cost worth bearing.

In the example just discussed, the hedger was concerned about the possibility of interest rates being higher in the future. It is, of course, possible that a firm will be concerned about interest rates being lower. For example, a firm may know that it will receive a substantial sum of money in three months' time. If the firm intends to lend this money it may be worried that interest rates will fall in the intervening period. In this situation the firm can hedge against a fall in interest rates by buying a futures contract. Thus futures can be used to 'lock in' interest rates when the firm is concerned about the possibility of higher or lower interest rates.

It is also possible for investors to protect themselves against movements in equity markets. This can be achieved by purchasing or selling futures contracts on the FTSE 100 share index. For example, an investment manager who is due to receive funds for investment in a few months will be concerned that the equity market will rise before the funds are available. The manager can hedge against such movement by buying FTSE 100 share index futures. In contrast, an investor concerned about falls in share prices can sell FTSE futures. However, the relationship between the futures price and the value of an investment portfolio will not be precise, as movements in the FTSE index will only approximate movements in the investor's portfolio (assuming the investor holds a diversified portfolio). The hedge will therefore be less than perfect.

Hedges are also likely to be less than perfect due to the fact that futures contracts are for a fixed unit of trading, and it is not possible to trade in parts of contracts. Thus, if you wish to hedge a rollover loan of £1.25m using the three-month sterling future you must either sell two contracts hedging £1m or three contracts hedging £1.5m. A perfect hedge is not possible in this case. Nevertheless, risk will be reduced by selling two or three contracts as compared to not selling any.

Clearly, this discussion of hedging is limited, but it should serve to demonstrate the benefits which futures contracts can offer to investors and to firms. Given the wide variety of financial instruments and commodities available, futures offer a range of possible forms of hedging for managers within firms.

CONCLUSION

In recent years futures contracts have come to play an increasingly important role in financial management. As well as providing some investors with the opportunity to speculate, they provide a very important means by which managers can hedge the risks they face. An increasing range of contracts are being developed, a recent innovation being property futures. Given the considerable uncertainty in the environment in which firms must operate, futures contracts are of considerable potential benefit to managers.

FURTHER READING

Heywood, J. (1984) *Using the Futures, Forwards and Options Markets*, A. & C. Black, London.

Redhead, K. (1990) *Introduction to Financial Futures and Options*, Woodhead-Faulkner, Cambridge.

Tucker, A.L. (1991) *Financial Futures, Options and Swaps*, West, St. Paul.

CHAPTER NINE

Options markets

INTRODUCTION

Over the last twenty years options markets have come to play an increasingly important role as a means of risk management. While trading in options has taken place for many years, it was not until 1973 that the first organized market for share options was created with the setting up of the Chicago Board Options Exchange. In 1978 the London Traded Options Market (LTOM) was opened on the floor of the International Stock Exchange in order to trade in share options. 1978 also saw the creation of the European Options Exchange in Amsterdam. Four years later the London International Financial Futures Exchange (LIFFE) was opened, which, in addition to trading in futures contracts, also offers traded options on financial instruments and currencies. These developments were largely a response to the unstable world economic climate in the 1970s and early 1980s, which led firms to demand risk-sharing and hedging instruments to lessen the effects of the volatility of, for example, interest rates and exchange rates. Thus, while options markets have been criticized for encouraging unnecessary speculation, they do in fact provide a means by which managers can reduce the risks associated with decision-taking in an uncertain world.

The growth in organized options markets has been accompanied by a transformation in the understanding of the factors relevant to the pricing of options. The most significant developments in option pricing theory were made by Black and Scholes (1973), since when the theory has been modified and extended.

Anyone attempting to gain an understanding of options for the first time is faced with the not inconsiderable task of trying to master a new terminology which is both extensive and, at times, bewildering. This chapter explains what an option is, what factors determine the price of an option, and why options markets are important, from the point of view of the manager, the individual investor, and society. As such the intricacies of various trading strategies are not discussed and hence many of the more perplexing terms associated with options markets are avoided. In addition, the primary concern here is with options associated with ordinary shares, although much of what will be said also relates to other options, such as options on stock indices, foreign currencies, commodity futures, and so forth.

THE NATURE OF OPTIONS

What is an option?

An option contract gives the holder of the contract the option to buy or sell shares at a specified price on or before a specific date in the future. The buyer of the contract pays the writer (or seller) for the right, but not the obligation, to purchase shares from, or sell shares to, the writer at the price fixed by the contract (the striking or exercise price). If there is provision in the contract for the option to be exercised at any time between writing and expiration, the option is known as an American option. If it can only be exercised on the expiration date, it is known as a European option. Essentially there are two types of options: a call option and a put option.

Call options

A call option gives the buyer the right to buy a fixed number of shares in a particular security at the exercise price up to the date of expiration of the contract. The writer of a call contract must sell shares in the underlying security to the buyer of the call at the agreed price if the buyer decides to exercise the option, that is, if the buyer calls for the shares.

Put options

A put option gives the buyer the right to sell a fixed number of shares in a particular security at the exercise price up to the date of expiration of the contract. The writer of a put contract must buy shares in the underlying security from the buyer of the put at the agreed price if the buyer decides to exercise the option, that is, if the buyer puts the shares to the writer.

For both types of option, contract buyers will only exercise the option if it is in their interests to do so.

The unit of trading

One of the fundamental characteristics of options markets is that there is a standard unit of trading. One contract is the minimum unit on which options can be traded. In the UK, one contract for share options normally represents 1000 shares of the underlying security, although for those shares with a relatively high price, say in excess of £10 (these are typically the shares of foreign companies), a contract may represent 100 shares. A US options contract represents 100 shares. Similarly, there are standard contract sizes for other types of options. It is not possible to trade in fractions of contracts, so most trading in UK share options must be in multiples of 1000 shares. Once written, the options contracts themselves can be bought or sold, and prices are therefore quoted for options contracts. The LTOM has now merged with LIFFE, through which trading in the UK takes place.

The Option Cycle

All options contracts are for a specified period of time, with share options having a life of three, six, or nine months. When options on a particular share are introduced they are allocated to a particular cycle:

January, April, July, October;

or February, May, August, November;

or March, June, September, December.

An option allocated to the first cycle, for example, will always have expiry dates in either January, April, July, or October. Since the maximum life of an option is nine months, only three of these expiry dates will be quoted at any one time for any particular share option.

The premium

The price of a traded option is known as the premium and is normally shown in terms of an option on a single share in the underlying security. Since more than one option contract may be traded at any time, a range of premiums will exist. Table 9.1 shows the premiums for options on ICI shares, as reported in the *Financial Times* on 8 July 1994.

Table 9.1

			Calls			Puts	
Option	*EP*	*Jul.*	*Oct.*	*Jan.*	*Jul.*	*Oct.*	*Jan.*
			Premium			Premium	
ICI	750	31.0	48.5	65.0	7.5	29.5	37.0
(*771)	800	7.5	25.0	41.0	35.0	58.5	65.0

Notes *Underlying security price
EP = Exercise price
Source: Financial Times, 8 July 1994

This table shows, for example, that buying a July 750 call option would cost £310 (31 × 1000). This would give the buyer the right to purchase 1000 ICI shares for £7.50 per share up to the expiry date in July. Clearly the premium will be determined for market forces. The factors which determine the value of an option are discussed later in the chapter.

OPTION STRATEGIES

From the discussion so far, it can be seen that there are four basic options positions which an individual can take:

1. Buy a call option;
2. Write a call option;
3. Buy a put option;
4. Write a put option.

If only one of these alternatives is undertaken at any one time and no shares are held in the underlying security, then the individual takes on a 'naked' position. Obviously, by combining some of these alternatives, for example by buying a call and writing a call, or by combining one or more of these alternatives with the purchase or sale of shares, fairly complex positions can be established.

The returns associated with the four basic 'naked' positions are shown in Figures 9.1–9.4. The diagrams demonstrate one of the major advantages of buying share options, namely that the possible losses associated with buying an option are limited to the cost of that option, whereas the potential profits are almost unlimited. For example, in the case of the ICI option, the maximum loss for the buyer of one July 750 call is £310. In contrast, if the price of the underlying security rose substantially, say to £10, the profit to the buyer of the call would be £2190 (the buyer of the call would have 1000 shares worth £10 each and would have paid £7.50 per share plus the premium of £310. Hence, the profit is £10 000 − (£7500 + £310)), a return of £2190 for an investment of £310. Once the option has been purchased, no further losses can be incurred on that transaction.

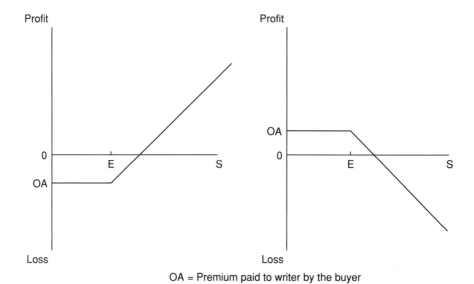

OA = Premium paid to writer by the buyer
E = Exercise price of the option
S = Price of the underlying security

Figure 9.1 Buy a call.   **Figure 9.2** Write a call.

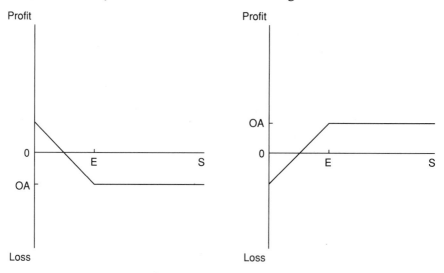

OA = Premium paid to writer by the buyer
E = Exercise price of the option
S = Price of the underlying security

Figure 9.3 Buy a put.   **Figure 9.4** Write a put.

In contrast, the potential profits to the writer of an option are limited to the premium received, whereas the potential losses are almost unlimited. (Actually, the profits and losses on put options are limited by the fact that the price of the underlying security cannot fall below zero.) The diagrams illustrate one other important aspect of options: they show that the profits and losses for the buyer of an option are the exact inverse of those for the writer of that option. In other words, options are a zero sum game.

WHY TRADE IN OPTIONS?

It is now appropriate to turn to the question of why investors buy and write call and put options. Consideration will only be given to the most basic of reasons here, leaving discussion of the less obvious advantages of buying and writing to a later section. Firstly, investors buy call options in the belief or expectation that the price of the underlying security will rise in the near future. In buying call options the individual is able to participate in any profits associated with a rising security price, while at the same time not committing large sums of money to the transaction. For example, an individual who on 8 July, believed that ICI shares would rise in price to £8.50, faces two alternatives by which to benefit from the expected rise. It is possible to either buy an option, for example the July 750 option for £310, or buy the underlying security. However, to purchase an equivalent number of shares to the number associated with an option (1000), the investor would have to commit £7710 (£7.71 × 1000). If the price of the underlying security does rise to £8.50, the investor who has purchased the option can then either sell the option, which will have increased in price to at least £1.00 (£8.50 − £7.50) and realize a minimum profit of £690 (£1000 − £310), or exercise the option. If the latter course of action is taken, the investor must pay the writer £7500 and can then sell the shares for £8500, realizing a profit of £690 (£8500 − (£7500 + £310)). The former course of action is simpler, is likely to involve lower transaction costs, and does not require the committing of the larger sum of money.

Writers of call options typically sell options on shares that they already own. The primary reason for doing this is the expectation that the underlying security price will be relatively stable, or may fall. Consider an investor who owns 1000 ICI shares which have a current price of £7.71. The investor sees that ICI January 800 have a premium of 41p a share. If the investor believes that the underlying security price is unlikely to go above £7.71 for some time, a January 800 call contract may be issued, yielding £410 (41 × 1000). At the expiry data there are three possible outcomes.

1. If the share price has risen above £8.00, the option is likely to be exercised. The writer will receive £8.00 per share, but has already received 41p per share, so the total received per share is £8.41.
2. If the share price is largely unchanged and at expiration stands between £7.71 and £8.00, it is unlikely that the option will be exercised and the writer has made a profit of £410.
3. If the share price has fallen, it is unlikely that the option will be exercised. While the writer's shares are now worth less, the 41p per share premium received for writing the call option compensates the writer for the loss on the shares. Only if the share price falls by more than 41p to below £7.30 will the loss on the shares be greater than the premium received on writing the option.

Clearly, then, a large rise in the price of the underlying security is required before the writer makes a loss; in the example above, the price would have to rise above £8.41. At the same time, writing a call provides protection against a fall in the price of the underlying security.

As was the case with call writing, investors buy puts in the expectation that the price of the underlying security may fall. Consider an investor who believes that ICI shares are over-valued at £7.71 and expects them to fall substantially in the near future, say to £7.00. The investor is able to buy an October

750 put for £295 (29.5p × 1000). If the share price does fall to £7.00, the put holder will be able to buy 1000 shares for £7000 and then put the shares to the writer at a price of £7.50 per share. Hence, the put holder will have made a profit of £205 (7500 − (£7000 + £295)) in a falling market. Alternatively, put buying can be used as a hedge against a fall in the price of shares already owned by an investor. If an investor holding 1000 ICI shares believes that the price is about right, but is worried that the price may fall in the future, it would be possible to buy an October 800 put for £585 (58.5p × 1000), thus ensuring a minimum gross selling price of £8.00. This is equivalent to a minimum net price of £7.415 (£8.00 − 58.5p). The investor is therefore hedging against a large fall in the share price, while at the same time only risking the loss of £585.

Put writing is undertaken by investors who expect the price of the underlying security to remain stable or rise – in other words, similar expectations to those of the call buyer. If the market does rise then writers of puts will have increased their profits. For example, an investor believes that ICI shares are undervalued at £7.71. By writing an October 750 put investors can receive £295 and will only have the shares put to them if the price should fall below £7.50, that is, if the price moves counter to the writer's expectations.

It is evident from the preceding discussion that, while buying and writing options can be viewed as being speculative in some situations, options markets can be used to manage the risk which an ivnestor faces, rather than increasing the risk faced. By writing a call option or buying a put option, investors can reduce their exposure to risk at a price which they believe to be acceptable. On the other hand, the buyer of a call option or the writer of a put option takes on extra risk in return for the possibility of increased gains. The options markets are thus balancing out the gains and losses associated with possible share price movements by redistributing the risk inherent in investment. The use of options for risk management will be looked at in more detail later in the chapter.

THE PRICING OF OPTIONS

As is the case with the underlying share, the price of the option is determined by the market forces of supply and demand. This section examines the factors which affect supply and demand, and hence determine the price of an option.

Intrinsic value and time value

It is, perhaps, easiest to understand the valuation of option contracts by viewing an option price as consisting of two component parts, the 'intrinsic value' and the 'time value'. The intrinsic value represents the actual financial benefit which will acrue to the contract holder if the option is exercised, that is, the difference between the price of the underlying security and the exercise price. A call option has intrinsic value if the price of the underlying security is greater than the exercise price. When this occurs the call option is 'in-the-money'. On the other hand, a put option has intrinsic value and is 'in-the-money' when the exercise price is greater than the price of the underlying security. The relationship between the intrinsic value (IV), the exercise price (EP), and the share price (S) are summarized below, together with the relevant terminology.

	Call options	*Put options*		
If	S > EP	S < EP	then	IV > 0 and option is 'in-the-money'.
If	S = EP	S = EP	then	IV = 0 and option is 'at-the-money'.
If	S < EP	S > EP	then	IV < 0 and option is 'out-of-the-money'.

The time value of an option represents the amount that options buyers are willing to pay, over and above the intrinsic value. Options have time value because in the time between the purchase of the option and its expiration, the price of the underlying stock may change in a way favourable to the option holder. Obviously, the option holder hopes that in this time an option which is currently either out-of-the-money or at-the-money will move into-the-money, or that an option which is currently in-the-money will move deeper into-the-money. The longer the time to expiration, the greater the time value of the option. This is evident in the premiums shown in Table 9.1 for ICI options. For the ICI 750 call options, the intrinsic value is 21p (current share price (£7.71) minus exercise price (£7.50)), while the time values for the July, October, and January options are 10p, 27.5p, and 44p respectively (the premium minus the intrinsic value). The 800 options have no intrinsic value because the share price is below the exercise price, and hence the premium on these represents only time value.

What determines an option's price?

Having identified the two aspects of the option price, consideration can be given to the factors likely to affect the price of an option. In order to keep the discussion at a fairly simple level, only the pricing of a European call option for which no dividend payments will be made during its life will be considered. Attempts to identify the factors which affect option prices have a long history. For example, as early as 1900, Bachelier developed a model for valuing options. However, it was not until the work of Black and Scholes in 1973 that a complete and acceptable option pricing model was developed. Black and Scholes developed a formula for valuing options, under several simplifying assumptions. While it is not possible in the confines of this chapter to give a rigorous exposition of their work, it is possible to identify and discuss the major implications of their formula.

The Black-Scholes formula demonstrates that the price of an option is determined by five major factors, as follows:

1. The current price of the underlying security;
2. The exercise price of the option;
3. The time to expiration;
4. The volatility of the share price;
5. The level of interest rates.

The way in which each of these factors will affect the price of an option will now be examined.

(1)   The relationship between the price of the underlying security and the price of the option is such that a rise in the share price will lead to an increase in the call price. The reason for this is that if the option is in-the-money, then an increase in the share price will move the option further into-the-money, thereby increasing its intrinsic value. Alternatively, if the call is out-of-the-money, an increase in the share price is likely to increase the time value of the option, since the option will be nearer to being in-the-money, and hence in the time to expiration is more likely to move into-the-money. However, an option which is a long way out-of-the-money is unlikely to show much (or even any) appreciation if the share price movement is small.

(2)   The higher the exercise price of the call, the lower the value of the option. The reason for this is much the same as that discussed for the relationship between the security price and the option value. Looking again at Table 9.1, it can be recalled that the July 750 call has an intrinsic value of 21p. If there were a July 760 call available its intrinsic value would be only 11p (£7.71 − £7.60). Both options would be in-the-money, but the one with the lower exercise price is deeper in-the-money and hence has a higher intrinsic value. An out-of-the-money option only has time value. However, the higher the exercise price is above the security price, the less likely the option is to move into-the-money. Hence the negative relationship between the exercise price and the value of the option.

(3)   The longer the time to expiration of the option, the greater will be the value of that option. This follows from the fact that the option will have greater time value. The nearer the time to maturity, the lower the time value, since there is less time for the security price to move in a favourable direction.

(4)   A share is said to be volatile if it has a history of large movements in price. Such a share is more likely to have large price movements in the future than is a share with little past volatility. Hence, it is more likely that the share price will move

in a way that makes the option profitable, or more profitable. Therefore, an increase in share price volatility will lead to an increase in the price of the call. It is recognized that a volatile share is also more likely than other shares to have a greater fall in price. However, call options are bought in the belief or expectation that the underlying security will rise in price, and it is this expectation which affects option prices.

(5)   An increase in interest rates will lead to an increase in the price of an option. The reason for this is that the buyer of the call has contracted to pay a given sum of money in the future if the call is exercised. Clearly, the present value of the exercise price will be lower the higher the rate of interest. This is easily understood if we consider that the call buyer invests the money which will be required in the event of exercising the option in an interest-bearing account. A rise in interest payments will increase the value of a given amount of money invested, and hence a smaller investment will be required to yield the necessary funds for exercising the option. In other words, higher interest rates have the same effect as a lower exercise price.

THE SIGNIFICANCE OF OPTIONS

The question of whether options markets are beneficial from society's point of view is an important one, given the arguments put forward by opponents of these markets. In particular, options have been criticized for encouraging unnecessary speculation. Perhaps the most important consideration here is that options markets can be of benefit even to individuals who are not active in the markets.

The role of security markets

In order to understand the significance of options it is helpful to recap the main functions of securities markets, which is to transfer funds between different participants in the markets, and to allow the participants to rearrange their consumption/

use of resources through time. Efficient securities markets lead to individual investors rearranging their consumption patterns, and to the users of funds (mainly firms) being able to undertake profitable productive opportunities which they may not otherwise have been able to undertake. In order for the securities markets to allocate resources efficiently, it is necessary for all relevant information to be incorporated into security prices. The prices of the securities themselves are an important source of information on which to make decisions regarding resource allocation.

Complete markets

The great problem faced by decision-makers is that the future is uncertain. However, the more securities are available, the more likely it is that participants in the market can make contingencies for the effects of uncertainty. In the extreme, it is possible to imagine a 'complete' market, where there are so many securities available that it would not be possible to create an additional security offering a new set of returns in various states of the world, that is to say, the security's returns could be duplicated by a portfolio of existing securities. In complete securities markets it is possible to remove all uncertainty regarding the value of the investor's future wealth. In practice, however, complete markets are not possible. The problems of drawing up contracts which cover all possible contingencies, and which are enforceable, are numerous and are associated with considerable transaction costs. While all contingencies cannot, in practice, be taken into account, it is nevertheless possible to issue securities which cover some of the possible contingencies.

Complete markets are desirable since they provide investors with maximum choice. However, more importantly from society's point of view is the fact that a complete market is necessarily Pareto-efficient, whatever the preferences of investors: in a complete market it would not be possible to make one investor better off, without making another investor worse off. Incomplete markets may be Pareto-efficient, but in some circumstances will not be.

Complete markets are impractical, but completeness can be approached by having additional securities. Options are one way of expanding the opportunities open to investors at relatively low transaction costs. Hence, options markets may be one way in which we can move securities markets towards completeness. Indeed, Cox and Rubinstein (1985) demonstrate that a full set of options can be equivalent to a full set of state-contingent claims.

It is also the case that options markets provide an additional source of information to decision-makers, and hence may be an aid to efficiency in securities markets generally. Thus, investors in the securities markets may benefit from the existence of options markets even when they themselves do not trade in options.

Options markets and investors

It is a well-established fact that in an efficient capital market, investors should not 'hold all their eggs in one basket'; they should hold a well-diversified portfolio. This must be borne in mind in the consideration of options. Options markets offer investors another investment opportunity, a further opportunity to diversify, but they should not be held in isolation. Bearing this in mind, it is possible to identify three main categories of reasons why investors might choose to hold options in their portfolio.

Option returns

It is possible that options will offer a pattern of returns that cannot be obtained by any combination of other assets. While in some circumstances it may be possible to duplicate the returns offered by options by holding a portfolio of shares and bonds, there will be other circumstances where this is not the case. For example, if the volatility of a share's price were to change unexpectedly, a call would increase in value. However, it is possible that the price of the underlying security is unaffected by such a change. Hence, the returns on the option have changed, while those on the share have not. Additionally, even in circumstances where the returns on an option can be duplicated, it is likely that it will be necessary to have a very active investment strategy, involving constant changing of the portfolio. Such a strategy obviously has considerable associated transaction costs, which will not be incurred by buying the option.

Furthermore, there will be circumstances when an investor in options can make returns superior to those offered by a share and bond portfolio of the same risk. This can occur when an investor possesses specialist information. Obviously, this requires some inefficiency in investment markets, but it is possible that options markets may be inefficient even when the market for the underlying security is efficient. In these circumstances, options may offer some investors superior risk-adjusted rates of return.

It can also be noted that options may offer borrowing and lending opportunities at rates preferable to those available else-where. As mentioned above, in some circumstances it is poss-ible to duplicate the returns offered by options by holding a portfolio of shares and bonds (that is to say, shares and bor-rowing/lending). Thus, implicit in options trading is an element of borrowing or lending. Since the rates of interest for the borrowing/lending implicit in options are largely deter-mined by large market participants (those benefiting from 'economies of scale'), they are likely to be preferable to the rates available to the small investor. Hence, implicitly borrowing or lending via the options markets may be preferable to holding a portfolio of shares and bonds.

Hedging

If a share's price increases in volatility, then holders of that share will incur extra risk, and investors may feel it necessary to sell some shares to reduce the risk faced. However, they are also forgoing potential profits, since the shares may rise substantially. An investor holding both shares and options can nevertheless hedge against the change in volatility, since the increased volatility will increase the value of the option. Hence, any potential profits forgone by selling shares at this stage to reduce risk will be partly offset by the increase in value of the option. Similarly, options can be used to hedge against unexpected changes in dividend policies of firms.

Institutional considerations

Margin trading is where securities are bought on credit, typically by paying a relatively small percentage of the purchase or selling price. However, margin traders are normally limited in the amount of borrowing they can undertake and typically must offer some collateral. Options trading can be used as an alternative to margin trading, yet the restrictions are much less severe for the options trader. Similarly, restrictions on short sales can be avoided by taking an equivalent position in options. Additionally, in some circumstances tax advantages may arise as a result of options trading. However, in order to understand these potential advantages it is necessary to have a good understanding of both tax laws and fairly complicated options strategies. Such considerations are beyond the scope of this chapter.

The use of options by managers

In addition to the advantages which options offer investors, there are other factors which make options an attractive financial instrument to be used by managers. It was established earlier in the chapter that options can be used to hedge against risk. Clearly, in many business decisions managers face situations of risk. It has already been shown how share options can be used to balance out the gains and losses associated with possible share price movements by redistributing the risk inherent in investment. In this section we discuss further how options can be used by managers to reduce risk by focusing on options other than those on shares.

Essentially there are two types of options users, namely traders (sometimes referred to as speculators) and hedgers. Traders are those people who are willing to take on extra risk exposure in the hope of making profits. Hedgers, on the other hand, are risk averse, and use options as a form of insurance against unfavourable changes in prices or interest rates. Managers are clearly most likely to be concerned with reducing risk exposure by hedging.

By using options a manager can hedge against adverse movements in interest rates, currency rates, or share prices. For example, consider a company which intends to bid for a contract in dollars. The company will be concerned that sterling might appreciate and thus reduce its profit margin. Such a company could hedge against sterling appreciation in either the futures, forward, or options markets for currency. However, given that at this stage the company does not know whether its bid will be successful, it does not wish to be *obliged* to take up a particular currency position. Only options give the company the right, but not the obligation, to take up the position. By using options the manager can hedge against sterling appreciation, while risking only the option premium should the bid prove unsuccessful. Similarly, firms are able to hedge against adverse changes in interest rates. Clearly, any movements could be in a direction favourable to the company, in which case the option would not be exercised. Again, the only loss to the company is the premium paid for the option.

The extent to which options can provide insurance against risk is perhaps best illustrated by reference to the use of options to hedge against the failure of a firm's research and development programme. By holding a portfolio of securities and options which will pay off in the event of the failure of the R & D programme, the firm is able to hedge against such failure. While identifying a portfolio which would yield profits if the R & D programme fails may be time-consuming, it could prove to be time well spent, given the riskiness of many R & D ventures.

These examples of the use of options demonstrate the considerable potential of options for managers. Essentially, options provide the manager with the means to hedge against various types of risks encountered in the course of business. Such hedging is achieved at a cost which is fixed and known to the manager at the time of the purchase of the option, since losses on the option cannot exceed the premium paid.

CONCLUSION

While options have some very distinctive characteristics, which are difficult to appreciate on first consideration, they are playing a continually increasing role in capital markets. In addition to an increasing number of options on individual underlying securities being obtainable, more complex options are now also available, such as options on the FTSE 100 Index. It appears likely that options will play an increasing part in investment strategies in the coming years as investors become more acquainted with the peculiarities of the markets, and it is therefore crucial that managers have an understanding of their role and the opportunities which they offer.

FURTHER READING

Black, F. and Scholes, M. (1973) 'The Pricing of Options and Corporate Liabilities', *Journal of Political Economy*, 81, pp. 637–54.

Cox, J.C., and Rubinstein, M. (1985) *Options Markets*, Prentice-Hall, Englewood Cliffs, NJ.

Ritchken, P. (1987) *Options: Theory, Strategy and Applications*, Scott, Foresman and Co., Glenview, Illinois.

Index